EST. 2012

MULTICOLOUR.

PALETTE

Nº2

NEW RAINBOW-HUED GRAPHICS

Vivid, expressive, full of energy and strength.
Indulge yourself in the buoyancy of colour splashed over
a remarkable spectrum of graphic projects.

by

Viction:ary

Foreword

Colour is such a constant in our everyday lives. Its presence is evident in everything we see, taste, touch and experience. Colour provokes an incredibly diverse range of emotions and responses depending on its use or context. Understanding how to harness the power of colour in design is key as it can steer the message you want to portray.

An emotional response to colour is complicated by the fact that colour can elicit different reactions from different people. This subjectiveness is like our relationship with music; what pleases one person is unpleasant to another. Research has proven that each colour has associations with certain feelings and can create a mood. Think of the strong reaction to a Rothko or Ian Davenport painting. For one person the use of colour in these artists' work holds a meaning of beauty, for another it is habitual or illogical.

Taking this further, look at a generic colour like blue. To some it can evoke sadness, yet to me I think of blue skies, blue ocean and New Order's 'Blue Monday', all of which are uplifting notions. Understanding colour choices and the implied perceptions they carry can help in the creation of effective design and can strengthen the audience response to the work.

This emotional response contrasts with the research carried out into the science of colour. Chevreul, an eighteenth century French chemist, noted whilst working with tapestries that colours interacted with each other when placed side by side. When viewed alone these colours had different properties altogether. In pairing colours together he could subsume or enhance colours in relation to each other. The campaign SEA created for the paper company Fedrigoni, called 'The Art of Colour', played with this theory. Its pages are a series of die-cut concentric circles, cannily showcasing the vivid hues in the Sirio range in direct comparison with one another.

In theory, our scientific and emotional relationships with colour work together but in reality the two can rarely be separated from each other. What we see and experience, regardless of the science will provoke an individual response in all of us. What the science does is harness these feelings, allowing brands and design to use these colours to evoke a desired emotion from the viewer.

EST. 2012

MULTICOLOUR

PALETTE

N°2

NEW RAINBOW-HUED
GRAPHICS

Vivid, expressive, full of energy and strength.
Indulge yourself in the buoyancy of colour splashed over
a remarkable spectrum of graphic projects.

by

Viction:ary

Contributors

Alan Chu | Albert Ibanyez | Alex Dalmau | Anagrama | Andrea Ataz | Anymade Studio | Aoki | artless Inc. | Artworklove | Ascend Studio | Atipus | ATMO Designstudio & FELD | studio for digital crafts | Base Design | Bleed | Blok Design | boymeetsgirl | Brighten the Corners | Browns | Build | Bunch | Bureau Collective | carnovsky | Chris Golden | Claudiabasel | Craig & Karl | Daikoku Design Institute | Daisy Balloon | Derek Kim | Emmanuelle Moureaux Architecture + Design | ENZED | Fabio Novembre | Fanette Mellier | FRVR | Grandpeople | Happy F&B | Helmo | Hey | Heydays | Holt | I LIKE BIRDS | Igor Zimmermann | IS Creative Studio. | JJAAKK | Jonathan Finch | Kerstin zu Pan | Kontor Kontur | Kurppa Hosk | L2M3 Kommunikationsdesign GmbH | La Tigre | Le Creative Sweatshop | Leif Podhajsky | Lemongraphic | Liquorice Studio | Lo Siento | macmeier | Mad Keen Design & Art Direction | Matilda Saxow | Metaklinika | Midnight Rendez-Vous | Mind Design | Mutabor Design GmbH | My Wet Calvin | Paco Peregrín | Palatre et Leclere Architectes | Paolo Palma | Paul Sangwoo Kim | Penique productions | Pentagram | Post Projects | Present & Correct | Purpose | R.I.S. Projects | Raffinerie AG für Gestaltung | Raúl Iglesias & Jesús Latuff & Luis Novero | Raw Color | Resort Studio | Reynolds and Reyner | Sara Cwynar | SEA | Second Story Interactive Studios | Simon Laliberté | Studio Brave | Studio Dumbar | Studio Iknoki | Studio Laucke Siebein | Studio Lin | Studio mw | Studio wilfredtimo | Sueh Li Tan | Thomas Bræstrup | Thompson Brand Partners | Tim Wan | Toormix | TORAFU ARCHITECTS | Torsten Lindsø Andersen | Txell Gràcia Design Studio | ujidesign | viction:workshop ltd. | WAAITT™ | Wanja Ledowski | Your Friends | Zim&Zou

PALETTE 02:

MULTICOLOUR
NEW RAINBOW-HUED GRAPHICS

Published and distributed by
viction:workshop ltd.

viction:ary™

viction:workshop ltd.
Unit C, 7/F, Seabright Plaza, 9-23 Shell Street,
North Point, Hong Kong
Url: www.victionary.com   Email: we@victionary.com
www.facebook.com/victionworkshop
www.twitter.com/victionary_
www.weibo.com/victionary

Edited and produced by viction:ary

Concepts & art direction by Victor Cheung
Book design by viction:workshop ltd.

Cover image by Grandpeople
Limited edition of 100, Gicleé print by Grandpeople,
available for purchase at pollenprint.grandpeople.no

ISBN 978-988-19439-0-3
Printed and bound in China

"What the science does is harness these feelings, allowing brands and design to use these colours to evoke a desired emotion from the viewer."

—

Bryan Edmondson SEA

"Colour is unobtrusive. Like salt, it goes well with everything; and if used wisely, it can give concepts and graphics a great taste."

—

Richars Meza
IS Creative Studio.

In one of the books by photographer Sophie Calle, who took pictures of born blind people and asked them to describe their idea of beauty, one of the pages saw an image of a kid who never sees, sitting next to her responded, "Green is beautiful. Because every time I like something, I'm told it's green. Grass is green, trees, leaves, nature too... I like to dress in green."

I think many like me seldom perceive the merits of being able to see and tell colours apart. Unlike food which we can relish by smell, seeing and taste, in the words of Ian Paterson in *A Dictionary of Colour* (2003), colour is nothing without sight and sight is the only sense by which we can experience colour.

The great advantage that colour has against other elements, such as typography, illustration, photography, is that colour is an unobtrusive visual cue. Like salt, it goes well with everything; and if used wisely, it can give concepts and graphics a great taste.

In a sense, the way we use colour is related directly to our past experiences and culture. Take FANTONE, a union of the traditional Spanish fan and the famous PANTONE® colour guide which I initiated to honour one of the country's most popular fashion accessories with an appeal to the young. We worked so hard choosing the right gamma of colours to apply on it. We asked ourselves so many questions, like what do we want to say through this fan? What if we add a wider range of tones? Does it have to be an authentic depiction of the original colour guide? Which gamma should go first? How could it appear as a seasonal tone? et cetera. The result, now available as FANTONE blueish, represents the transition from summer heat to ice chill, with a blue tone spiced up with a little red.

In a nutshell, colour can add or take out meanings from many objects. As a designer, I feel we have a big responsibility for using colours as a powerful tool to make meanings on top of words and graphics and let it not go to waste.

Howard Smith Paper Graphic Design and Print Awards

Poster series mailed out monthly to promote and invite entries for the second Howard Smith Paper Awards. Taking European paper sizes as its inspiration, the last A0 poster concluded the campaign with the sizes successively aligned in multiple tones.

Browns
Client: Howard Smith Paper

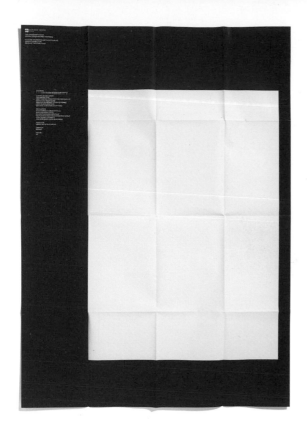
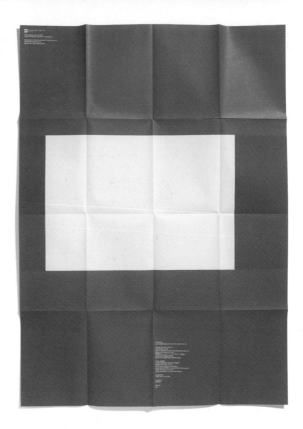
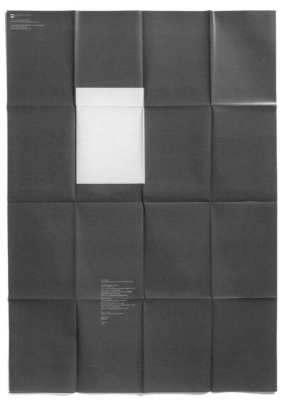

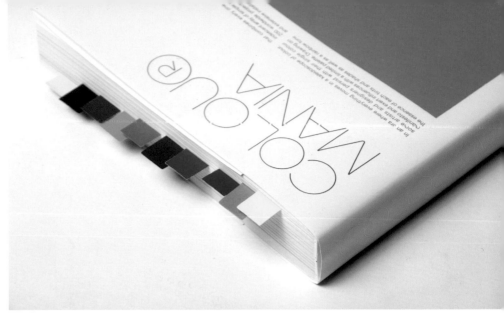

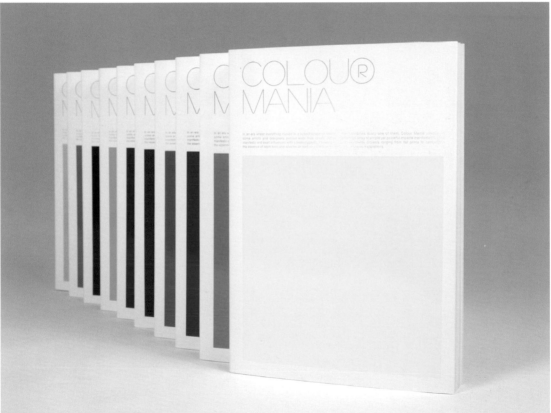

Colour Mania

Featuring a spectrum of unicolour projects, *Colour Mania*'s jacket coheres the theme with ten colour editions and an iridescent title. Small built-in tags sticking out at the book's top reveal a rainbow and function as section marks at once.

viction:workshop ltd.
Client: viction:ary

Folkets Hus Identity Program

Folkets Hus is a place offering rooms for multiple social functions,
such as conferences and exhibitions. Versatile, open and fun to use,
the identity program visualised various spatial forms in an array of
colourful blocks.

Aoki
Client: Folkets Hus (Gothenburg)

"Colour was important here to suggest 'many people'. We wanted the identity to look happy and extrovert."

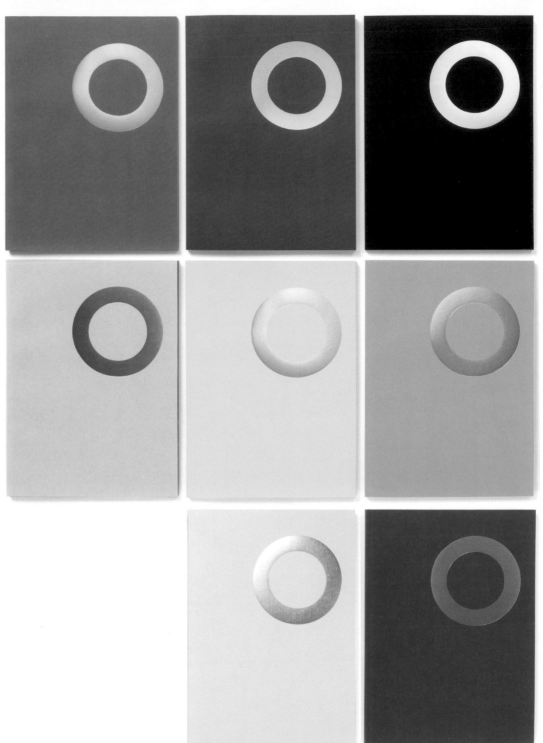

Circular

Launched as a platform for disparate love for type designs, Circular's 17th issue sees an unprecedented take, giving up all editorial space for typographic showcases with full bleed. Featuring a silver ring in place of its name, the issue comes in eight colour covers and a slipcase.

Pentagram

Client: Typogrphic Circle

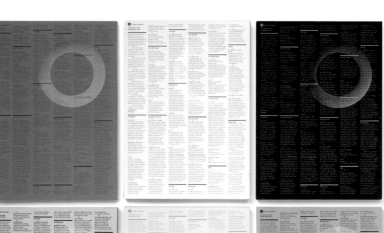

015

Elfriede Jelinek
Literaturnobelpreis 2004

Günter Grass
Literaturnobelpreis 1999
Nobel Prize in Literature 1999

Gerhart Hauptmann
Literaturnobelpreis 1912
Nobel Prize in Literature 1912

Theodor Mommsen
Literaturnobelpreis 1902
Nobel Prize in Literature 1902

Heinrich Böll
Literaturnobelpreis 1972
Nobel Prize in Literature 1972

Paul Heyse
Literaturnobelpreis 1910
Nobel Prize in Literature 1910

Nobel

Deutschsprachige
Literaturnobelpreisträger
*German speaking
Winners of the Nobel
Prize in Literature
1902–2004*

GOETHE-INSTITUT

Theodor Mommsen
Literaturnobelpreis 1902
Nobel Prize in Literature 1902

German-speaking Winners
of the Nobel Prize in Literature

The colourful spectrum of red celebrates 11 German-speaking winners of the Nobel Prize
in Literature with extracts of individual's work. A cardboard slipcase was devised to hold
all booklets together as they were distributed by the Goethe-Institut.

Brighten the Corners
Client: Goethe-Institut

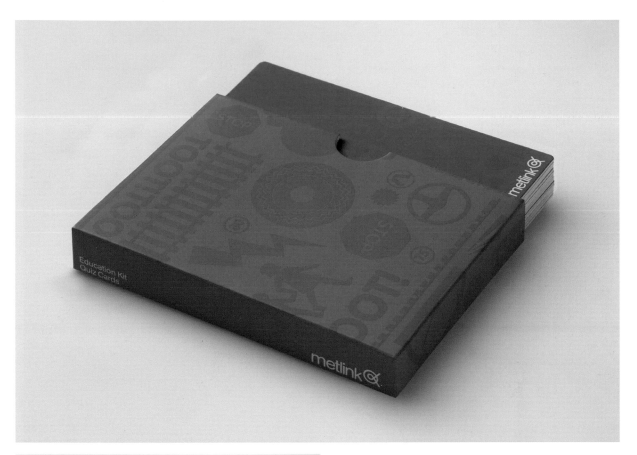

Metlink Education

While games facilitate learning, colours aid recognition. Adopting the transport network mode colours and illustrations, the education-cum-promotional kit enables primary school teachers to teach children about travelling by public transport in Melbourne.

Holt
Client: Metlink

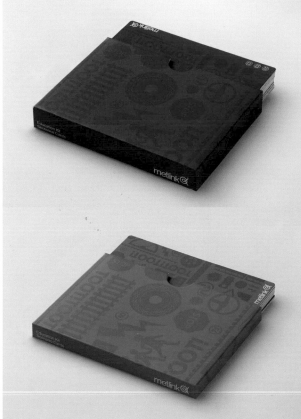

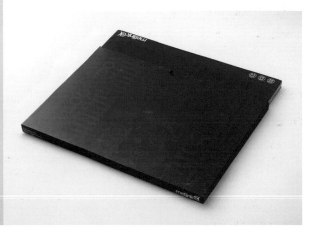

Toscatti

Toscatti is a new kitchenware brand with more than a dozen container models, varied in capacity and shapes. The packaging system eases up on consumers' search with shades indicating the models' characteristics and huge numbers for the size.

Anagrama
Photo: Carogafoto
Client: Wagner Brands

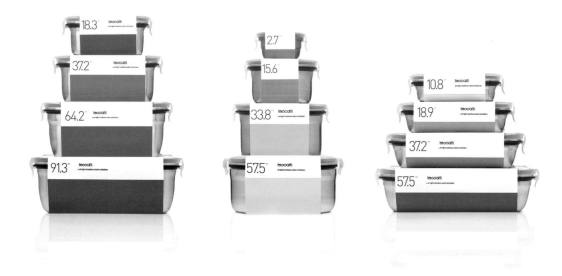

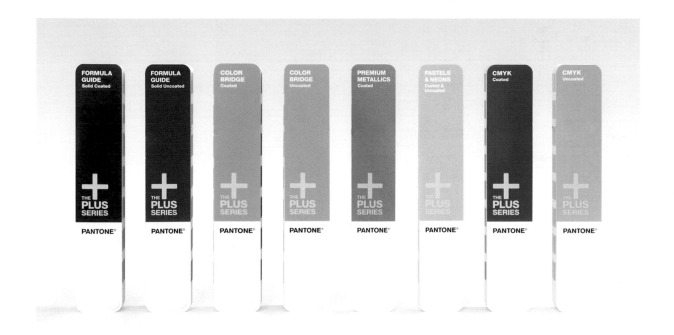

PANTONE® PLUS SERIES Book & Guides

Taking a unique colour from each of the PANTONE® PLUS SERIES systems, the
entire tool set is presented as a mini-guide comprised of enlarged colour chips.
Base's work spanned the collection's name, icon and packaging design.

Base Design

Photo: Maurice Scheltens, Liesbeth Abbens
Client: PANTONE®

PANTONE® PLUS SERIES Posters

To introduce PANTONE®'s new colours as good creative partners, Base pictures the series as "the building blocks for your next big idea". The studio has also conceived the line's name, icon and packaging for its chip books and set boxes.

Base Design

Photo / Props.: Maurice Scheltens, Liesbeth Abbens
Client: PANTONE®

THE BUILDING BLOCKS OF YOUR NEXT BIG IDEA

lus Series,
n fo the
System.

The Plus Series supercharges it with a host of new colors, features, and digital tools.

PANTONE®
pantone.com/plus

Introducing, The Plus Series, the next generation fo the Pantone Matching System.

The Plus Series supercharges it with a host of new colors, features, and digital tools.

"Colour is pure emotion and emotion is what moves people."

Revolver
14 Maddison Street
East Redfern NSW 2021
Telephone +61 2 9363 2122
Facsimile +61 2 9363 0522
www.revolverfilm.com

Directors
Tim Godsall
Bruce Hunt
Justin Kurzel
Simon McQuoid
Kris Moyes
Noam Murro
Steve Rogers
Glue Society
Aaron Stoller

1 - 500

Revolver

Known for its high-end TVC productions, Revolver's identity incorporates all things related to film making, from its typeface to its palette. In a set of seven, the individually designed directors' showreels appropriate the colours of film scripts which denote a change of roles.

Holt
Client: Revolver

Unity in Diversity

NIS has many faces but only one central design element — the diagonal derived from the logotype's N. Six colours are assigned to represent individual staff member and a console-style typography to reference the company's line of business.

boymeetsgirl

Printing: Keule Druck Berlin
Client: New Image Systems GmbH

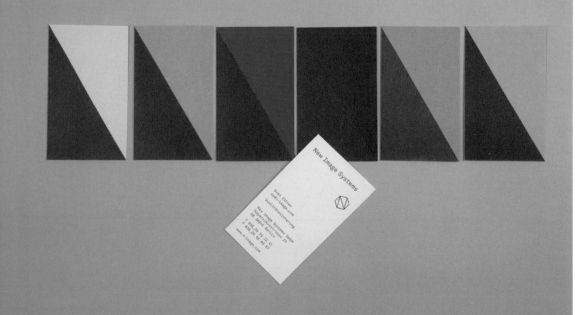

Vrrb

Vrrb Interactive is a California-based web-developing studio start-up. The identity is conceived using only a custom-made wordmark and colour papers, allowing for the broad colour range and minimum costs for production and colour quality control.

FRVR

Client: Vrrb Interactive

Beyond
Blue

National
Depression
Initiative

Providing a national
focus and community
leadership to increase the
capacity of the broader
Australian community to
prevent depression and
respond effectively.

We aim to build a society
that understands and
responds to the personal and
social impact of depression,
work actively to prevent it,
and improve the quality of
life for everyone affected.

www.beyondblue.org.au

Beyond Blue

Beyond Blue devotes itself to promote the awareness of depression and develop
prevention measures in Australia. The poster graphically portrays a sense of
hope in literally a spectrum of living, without (pure) blue and sadness.

Holt
Client: Beyond Blue

Polaroid Exhibition Collateral

Held at Centre for Contemporary Photography in Australia, Polaroid exhibition celebrated the impact instant film had on photography. The poster pays homage to the iconic colour bars in Polaroid's product identity developed by Paul Giambarba.

Holt

Client: Centre for Contemporary Photography (CCP) Melbourne

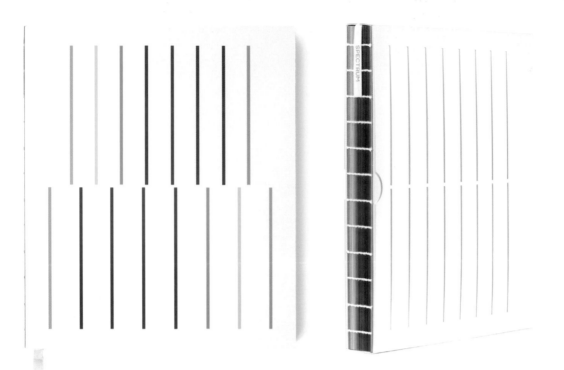

Spectrum

Colour is everything in this design. Titled *Spectrum*, the book lets colour speak for itself. Each spread displays a single colour along with its corresponding CMYK value, showcasing a full spectrum between the pages and on the spine as well.

JJAAKK

Designed in 2008
by Jesse Kirsch
School of Visual Arts
209 East 23 Street
New York, NY 10010

Copyright © 2008 Jesse Kirsch

10 20 19 8 · 15   First Edition

SPECTRUM / Jesse Kirsch

Printed on my Epson and assembled by hand.

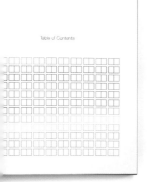

> "Colour is everything in this design. The book literally *IS* colour. Pure and true, let the colour speak for itself."

Table of Contents

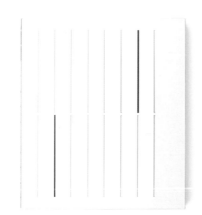

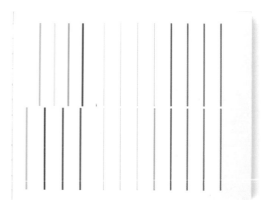

SPECTRUM
Designed by Jesse Kirsch

Atelier BangBang

BangBang is a screen-printing workshop and lab set to explore colour impact on paper and textile. The expressive power of colour was converted into a philosophy in various media, from packaging to corporate communication.

Simon Laliberté
*Special credits: Université du Québec à Montréal, UQAM,
Professor Louis Gagnon*

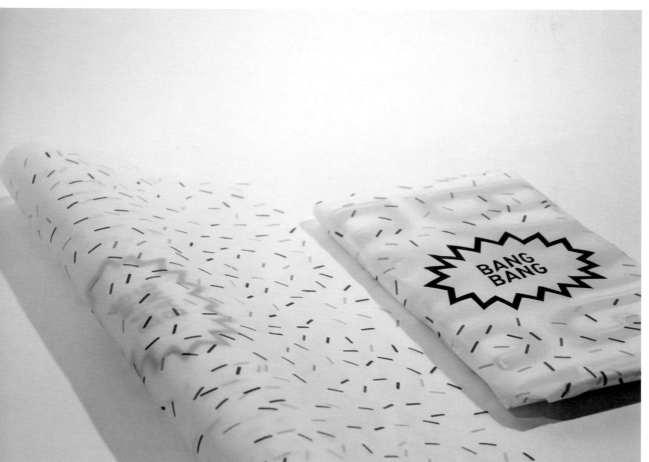

La Ciudad de las Personas

Aschewing black, the colour of fumes and asphalt, the participatory campaign covers the city with colours while inviting people to imagine a healthier city with less vehicles and spaces reserved for cars. Optimism was the base of the entire event.

Andrea Ataz

UN LUGAR
MÁS SANO

UN LUGAR
EN EL QUE
EL ESPACIO
ES DE TODOS

UN LUGAR DONDE
DISFRUTAR LA
DISTANCIA

UN LUGAR
MÁS HUMANO

UN LUGAR
DONDE ME
SIENTA LIBRE

UN LUGAR
QUE RESPETE
AL PLANETA

UN LUGAR DONDE
EL ASFALTO SE
CUBRA DE COLORES

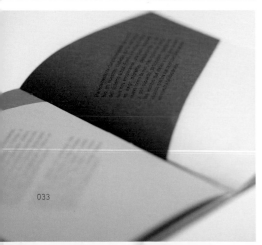

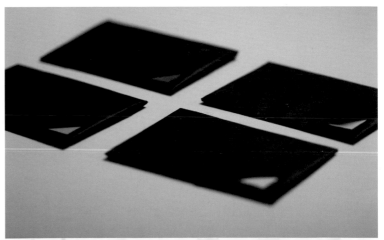

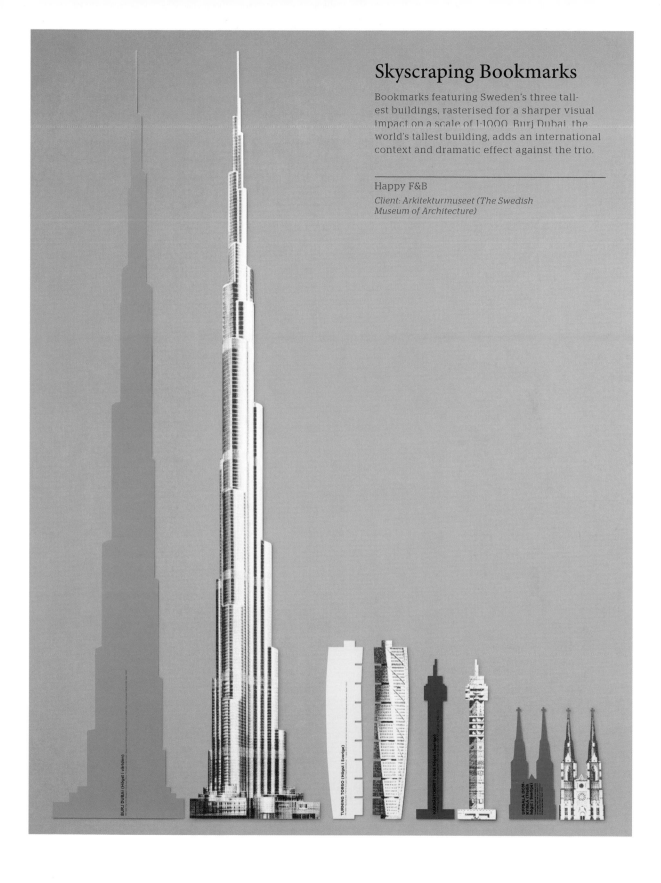

Skyscraping Bookmarks

Bookmarks featuring Sweden's three tallest buildings, rasterised for a sharper visual
impact on a scale of 1:1000. Burj Dubai, the
world's tallest building, adds an international
context and dramatic effect against the trio.

Happy F&B
*Client: Arkitekturmuseet (The Swedish
Museum of Architecture)*

Rítmia

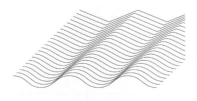

Rítmia. Music Therapy

Identity for social music therapist and educator Celia Castillo. The visual elements illustrate Castillo's very own rhythmic exercises, with a basic aim to provoke emotional responses in her patients.

Atipus

Client: Celia Castillo. Rítmia

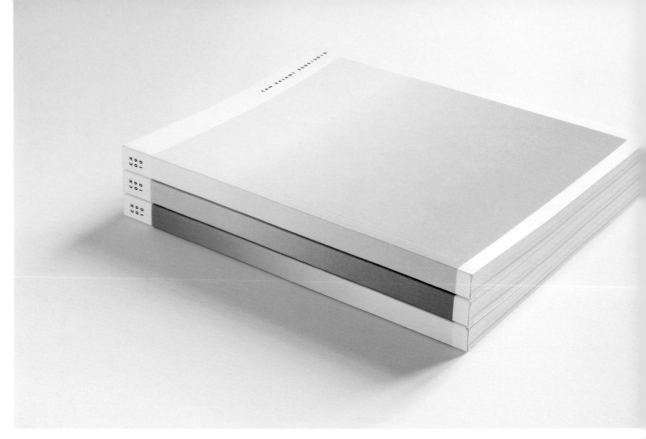

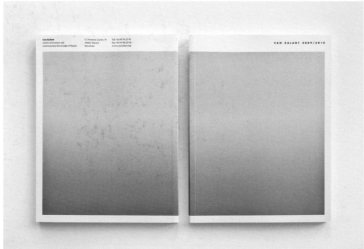

Annual Report for Can Xalant

Available in Catalan, Spanish and English, the annual reports recount what the arts centre realised during 2009/10. Colours here connote language and the three as a whole, on the covers and through the tinted images inside.

Albert Ibanyez

Client: Can Xalant (Centre for the Creation of Visual Arts and Contemporary Thought)

Can Xalant
Centre de Creación y Pensamiento
Contemporáneo de Mataró

C/ Francesc Layret, 75
08302, Mataró
Barcelona

Tel. +34 93 741 22 91
Fax +34 93 741 22 93
www.canxalant.org

CAN XALANT 2009/2010

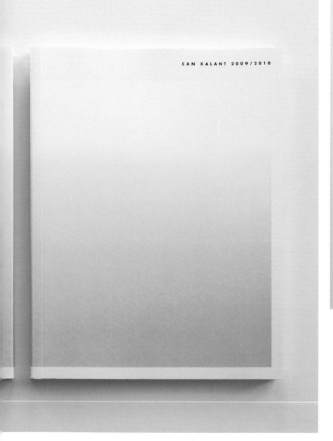

CAN XALANT 2009/2010

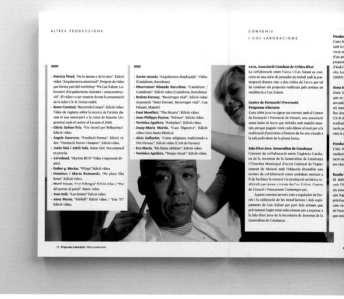

ALTRES PRODUCCIONS

CONVENIS
I COL·LABORACIONS

2009

· Patricia Ward, "De lo mismo y de lo otro". Edició
video "Arquitectura emocional". Projecte de vídeo
que forma part del workshop "We Can Xalant. La-
boratori d'arquitectures nòmades i autoconstruc-
ció". El vídeo va ser mostrat durant la presentació
de la ruKta CS-R. Unitat mòbil.
· Roser Caminal, "Recorrido Canoys". Edició-vídeo.
Vídeo de registre sobre la recerca de l'artista durant el seu intercanvi a la ciutat de Rosario (Ar-
gentina) amb el centre el Levante el 2008.
· Glòria Safont-Tria, "Un record per Pellestrina".
Edició vídeo.
· Àngela Guerrero, "Fundació Fenosa". Edició ví-
deo. "Fundació Duran i Sanpere". Edició vídeo.
· Jonàs Sala i Adrià Sala, Sense títol. Documental
en procés.
· Airvoland, "Skyline BCN" Vídeo i impressió di-
gital.
· Esther g. Mecías, "Wings" Edició vídeo.
· Domènec i Marta Ramoneda, "No place like
home" Edició vídeo.
· Maroi Anson, "Can Ethregas" Edició vídeo / "Per
del porter el penal". Retoc vídeo.
· Joan Solé, "Les Sontes" Edició vídeo.
· Anna Marín, "Mirleft" Edició vídeo / "Dar Tt"
Edició vídeo.

2010

· Xavier Arenós, "Arquitectura desplaçada". Vídeo.
(Canòdrom, Barcelona)
· Observatori Nòmada Barcelona, "Canòdrom /
Canòdrom". Edició vídeo (Canòdrom, Barcelona)
· Berfiem Estrany, "Recorregut vital". Edició vídeo
(exposició "Santi Estrany. Recorregut vital". Can
Palauet, Mataró)
· Dani Montlleó, "The Stuarts". Edició vídeo.
· Jean-Philippe Peynot, "Poèmes". Edició vídeo.
· Verònica Aguilera, "Parkplats". Edició vídeo.
· Josep-Maria Martín, "Casa Digestiva". Edició
vídeo (Arts Santa Mònica)
· Aleix Gallardet, "Cants religiosos tradicionals a
l'Alt Pirineu". Edició vídeo (CAN de Farnes)
· Eva Martín, "Els límits oblidats". Edició vídeo.
· Verònica Aguilera, "Temps viscut". Edició vídeo.

ACCA, Associació Catalana de Crítics d'Art
La col·laboració entre l'ACCA i Can Xalant es con-
creta en una sèrie de jornades de treball amb la par-
ticipació d'entre cinc a deu crítics de l'ACCA per tal
de conèixer els projectes realitzats pels artistes en
residència a Can Xalant.

Centre de Formació i Prevenció.
Programa Alterarte
L'any 2006 ja es va signar un conveni amb el Centre
de Formació i Prevenció de Mataró, una associació
sense ànim de lucre que treballa amb malalts men-
tals, perquè puguin venir cada dijous al matí per a la
realització d'activitats a l'entorn de les arts visuals a
la sala polivalent de la planta baixa.

Sala d'Art Jove. Generalitat de Catalunya
Conveni de col·laboració entre l'Agència Catalana de la Joventut de la Generalitat de Catalunya
i l'Institut Municipal d'Acció Cultural de l'Ajun-
tament de Mataró amb l'objectiu d'establir uns
termes de col·laboració entre ambdues entitats a
fi de facilitar la creació i la producció artística re-
alitzada per joves a través de Can Xalant, Centre
de Creació i Pensament Contemporani.

Aquest conveni serveix com a regulador de l'ac-
cés i la utilització de les instal·lacions i dels equi-
paments de Can Xalant per part dels artistes que
prèviament hagin estat seleccionats per a exposar a
la Sala d'Art Jove de la Secretaria de Joventut de la
Generalitat de Catalunya.

武蔵野美術大学

2011 入学試験問題集

JAPANESE PAINTING. PAINTING. PRINTMAKING.
SCULPTURE. VISUAL COMMUNICATION DESIGN.
INDUSTRIAL, INTERIOR AND CRAFT DESIGN.
SCENOGRAPHY, DISPLAY AND FASHION DESIGN.
ARCHITECTURE. SCIENCE OF DESIGN.

2012年

■ 一般入学試験
■ 公募制推薦、
■ 外国人留学生
■ 帰国生特別入学
■ 3年次編入学試
■ 大学院造形研究
■

Musashino Art University

New Year's Card 2012

Art-directed by Daigo Daikoku, Musashino Art University's new year cards and collateral for 2012 underlined the institute as a venue for creative ventures. The idea was further condensed into the beauty of colour, with feathered edges allusive to the immense potential for art and design.

Daikoku Design Institute
Photo: Shun Takano
Client: Musashino Art University

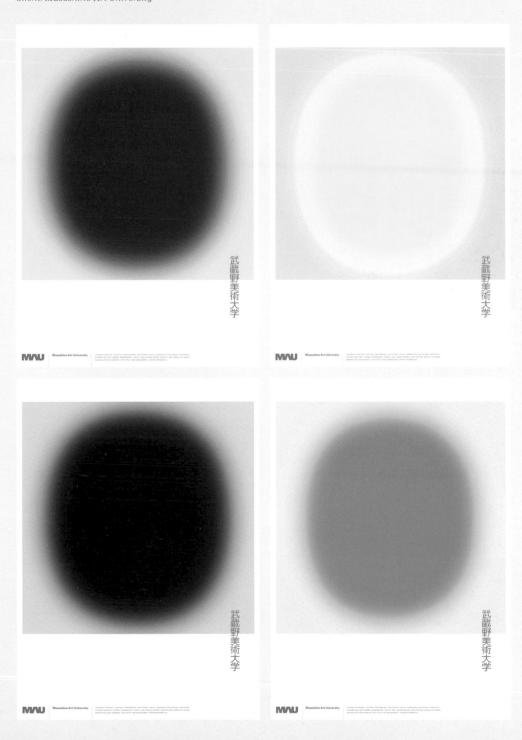

JACK
KEROUAC

ON
THE ROAD

PUBLISHER

Jack Kerouac Book Covers

Using a riotous profusion of colours, these new covers for Jack Kerouac's classic novels stress the American novelist's spontaneous prose without extravagance. The covers are Andersen's personal project.

Torsten Lindsø Andersen

"It's very hard to communicate colours. They easily attach moods to a certain brand or...destroy pretty much every beautiful piece of art or design, but life would be beyond boring without colours."

JACK KEROUAC

THE DHARMA BUMS

PUBLISHER

JACK KEROUAC

LONESOME TRAVELER

PUBLISHER

Shift Festival

Incorporated with an upwards arrow, the robust 'S' has been the spirit of Shift since its introduction by Claudiabasel. With a different theme every year, posters for Shift 2010 saw the idea of "Lost & Found", with new discoveries and interpretations in electronic arts.

Claudiabasel
Client: Shift

Bermellón Branding

Bermellón sets to take traditional Mexican flavours to premium confectionery experiences through refined recipes, handicrafts and packaging. Anagrama's proposal reflects the brand's sophistication in an elegant typographic palette and a family-monogram-like logotype.

Anagrama
Client: Bermellón

"The variety of gradients give us the chance to catch the eye, and be coherent with the brand's concept."

BERMELLÓN

LIGERA

BERMELLÓN

Architecture
PLB

Architecture PLB Identity

Architecture PLB is dynamic and happy to embrace changes as the logo
projects. Based on a single sign which continues to change colours and
rotate on different surfaces, the British firm tells clients that they will
welcome challenges with open arms.

SEA
Client: Architecture PLB

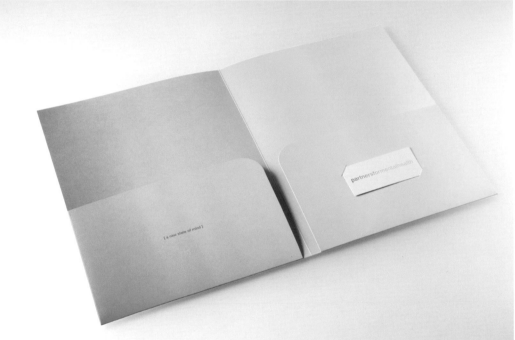

Partners for Mental Health

Apart from a new state of mind, the complexity of people's feelings is also at its core. Fresh as a daisy, the non-profit's new identity imparts hope, valour and resolve to improve Canada's mental environment for the mental health cause.

Blok Design
Client: Partners for Mental Health

Vitra Campus Summer Party

Introducing two events at Vitra's summer party in 2011, separate invites were conceived with yellowish and blueish colour bands that impart difference and continuity at once. When put together, the invites heightened the event like garlands.

L2M3 Kommunikationsdesign GmbH
Client: Vitra

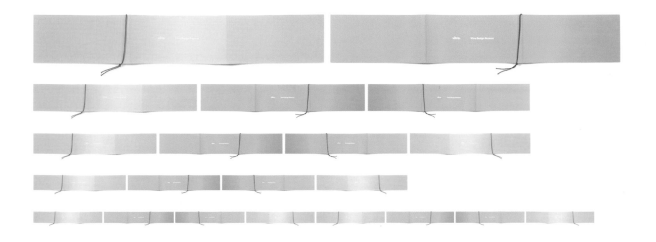

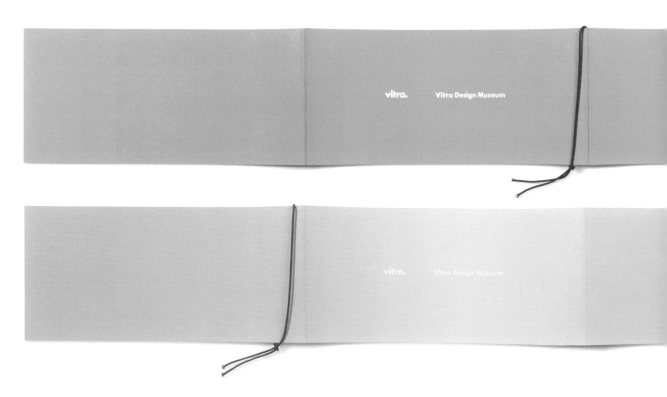

I'm An Office Worker

A book of everyday poetry, satire and tragedy based on a forum thread titled 'I'm an office worker' within music webzine Drownedin-Sound.com. Colour remarks on the user-friendly MS Word art tool that helps to make things "pop" in office documents.

Resort Studio

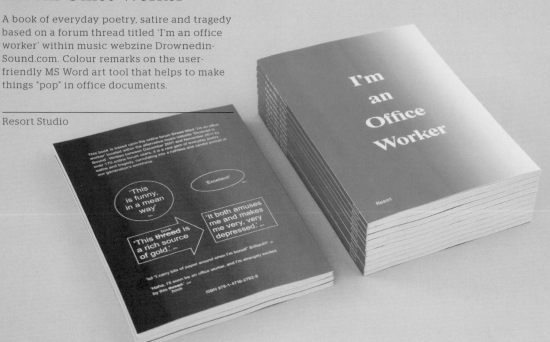

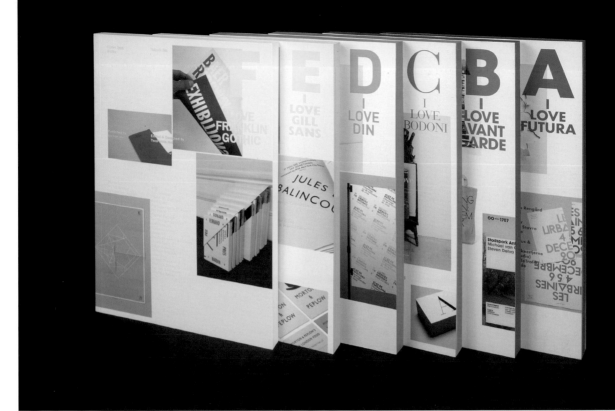

I Love Type

Focusing on one typeface at a time, *I Love Type* researches classic type design in modern visual culture. Tipping the edges and spines in neon inks, the design invite readers to complete the rainbow by amassing every member of the family.

viction:workshop ltd.

Editorial / Layout design: TwoPoints.Net
Client: viction:ary

Erwan Frotin Invitation

Invitation and portfolio package for Erwan Frotin's photo exhibition 'Flora Olbiensis' at Art+Commerce. The colour gradations airbrushed onto the edges convey the spirit of spring in Frotin's pictures of wild flowers captured in Hyères, France.

Studio Lin
Photo / Client: Art+Commerce

Liquorice Studio Brand Collateral

Liquorice's business card introduced the brand's new Liquorice 'Allsorts' palette. Each card features one 'Allsorts' colour sandwiched between two black layers with screenprinted details producing a tactile touch.

Liquorice Studio

Mutabor Corporate Design

From its name to the use of colour, Mutabor makes a clear and simple statement for their long-term resolution in making changes through innovation. "Mutabor" is derived from Latin and means 'I'm going to change'.

Mutabor Design GmbH

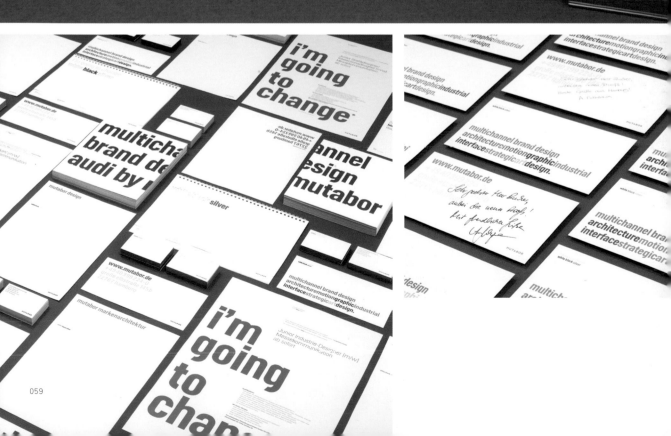

059

Fantone

The redesign of the PANTONE® colour guide is a tribute to the all-time popular Spanish fan with a youthful touch. Here, colour connects the youth with traditions, with a visual link to the iconic product of the times.

IS Creative Studio.

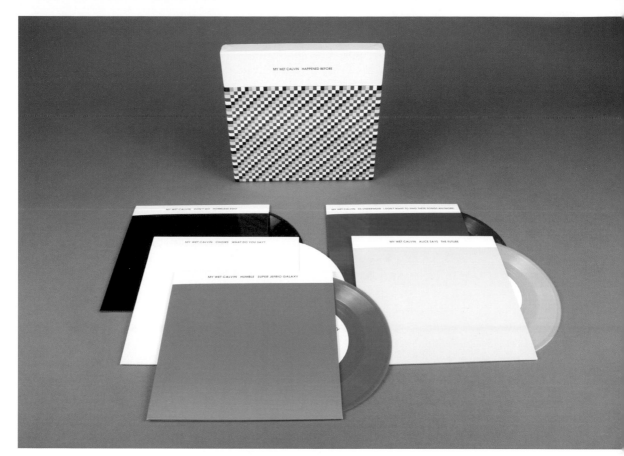

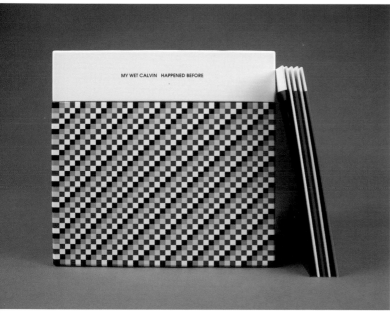

Happened Before

Happened Before is My Wet Calvin's latest singles collection produced in hands with five distinct producers. Colours was employed as the medium to depict the individuals, harmoniously woven into a strict grid pattern on the case and thus, the box set becomes whole.

My Wet Calvin
Client: Inner-Ear Records

Laus

Brochure and identity for the 40th Spanish Laus Design Awards. Hey's idea was an abstract campaign that reflected the passage of time. The strata of "L" from "Laus" on the front was laid out on multiple colour paper sheets to symbolise development and change.

Hey
Client: adg-fad

GRC Identity Program

GR Communications is a progressive PR agency comprised of five forward-thinking experts. The palette of five colours at once accents individuality and their different skill sets, yet as harmonious and vibrant as the closely knit team.

Ascend Studio
Client: GR Communications

Sirio by Fedrigoni

Named 'SIRIO, The Art of Color', the book sets off visual experience in relation to Chevruel's simultaneous contrast theory. Every turn of the page reveals a unique interplay between 21 colour sheets and an integrated view through its multiple apertures.

SEA

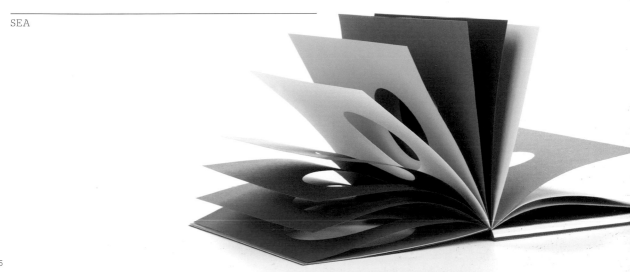

Dan!

Visual identity for percussionist Dan Arisa. The brand plays on the artist's monosyllabic name and visualise it as a sound, with rubber stamps to transform the printing process into a drum technique.

Alex Dalmau

Photo: Susana Gellida
Client: Dan Arisa

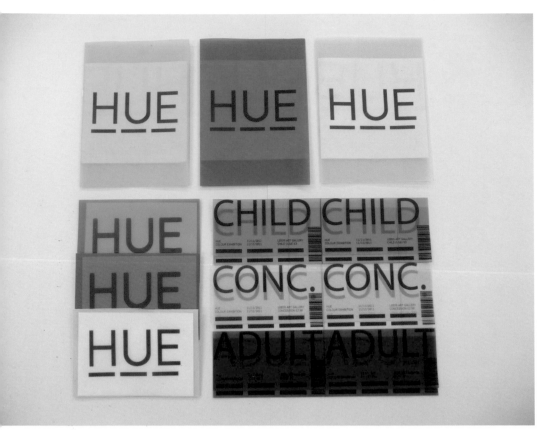

Hue: Colour Exhibition

Based around the concept of 'three', the promotional materials were Finch's personal project created for an exhibition based on colour. From its name 'HUE' to its colour base, the idea was consistent in each set of invites, tickets and guides.

Jonathan Finch

Una movida editorial

A collection of studies on magazines and publications released in the 70's and 80's in Spain. The intense palette speaks of the vibrant Spain around the era when the dictator's censorship ended, causing everyone to explore what was forbidden before.

Raúl Iglesias, Jesús Latuff, Luis Novero

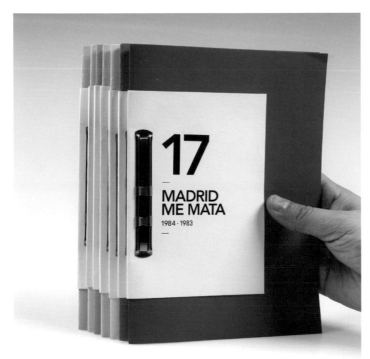 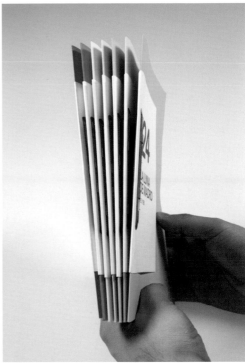

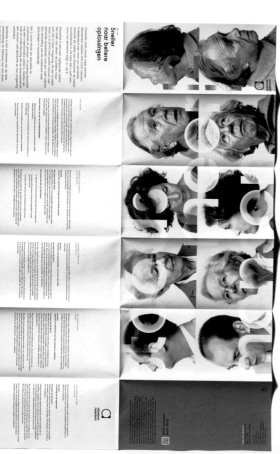

Alzheimer Nederland
Visual Identity

Alzheimer Nederland is a non-profit dedicated to the research and support of Alzheimer's disease and patients. Based on a bold and confident type, Studio Dumbar's identity design for AN visualises hopes and effects of dementia at once with vanishing points.

Studio Dumbar
Photo: Mathijs Labadie
Client: Alzheimer Nederland

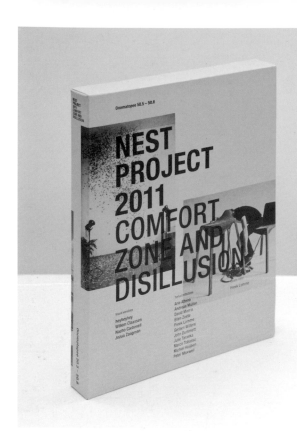

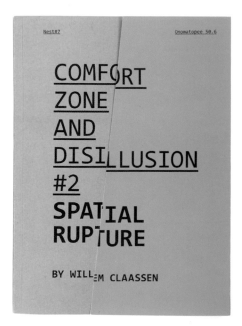

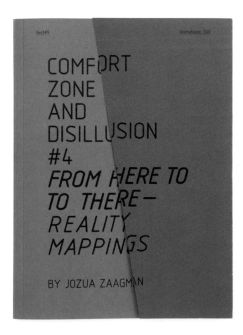

Nest 2011 Box - Onomatopee

Each year, Nest highlights emerging art and design talents, with one in each book. Entitled *Comfort Zone & Disillusion*, 2011's collection coheres 2010's concept with a slanted cover and mismatched colours and types to suggest how the artists work in an unadapted way.

Raw Color
Client: Onomatopee

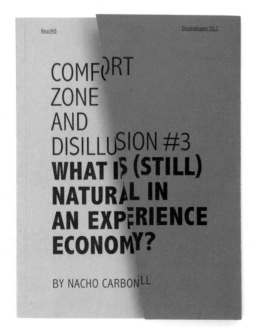

The Collection

The Collection is restaurant, cultural event and retail space with an identity taking references from multiple prints, limited editions and artist signatures. Screen-printing has allowed colour variations on the printing bed, making each print unique.

Mind Design
Client: The Collection

The owners of The Collection have combined their passion for food with their Mediterranean background to create dishes that pay homage to the very best produce of the "Olive Oil" countries of southern Europe. Using only olive oil in the cooking, instead of butter, the dishes are fresh and light.

The Collection is dedicated to using only the finest ingredients sourced from suppliers such as the award-winning Laverstoke Park and premium butchers, O'Shea's of Knightsbridge. The menu offers something for everyone, from light bites, as well as fresh fish and succulent meats cooked on the grill.

OD 2011

Aimed at Norwegian youth, Operation Day's 2011 campaign challenged the partial views many have on opportunities in Africa. The identity pictured the theme with strong contrasts between the negative and the positive through colours and types.

Heydays
Client: Operasjon Dagsverk (OD)

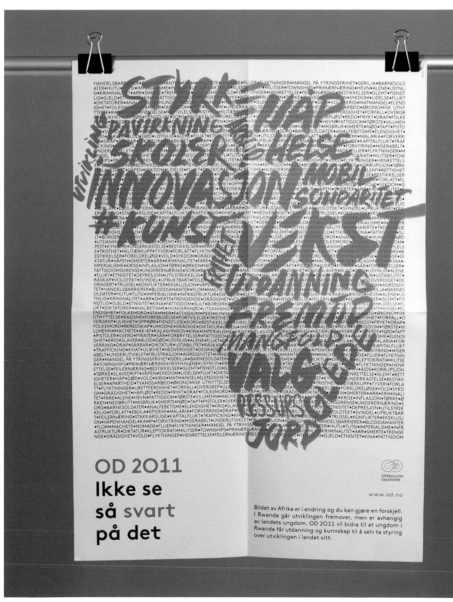

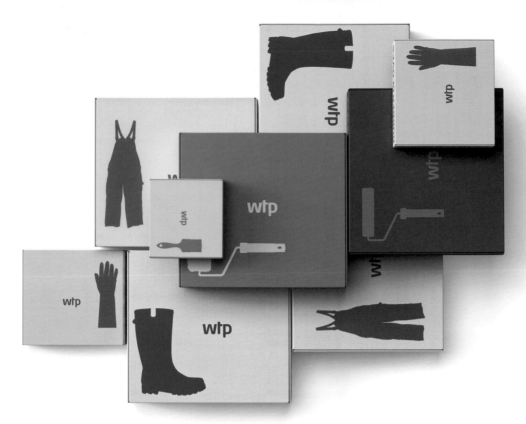

Waldo Trommler Paints

New to the US market, the Finnish paint manufacturer believes "looking different" is the first step to win. Every item is a bright and memorable combination of colours and objects that all together build the entire brand.

Reynolds and Reyner
Client: Waldo Trommler Paints

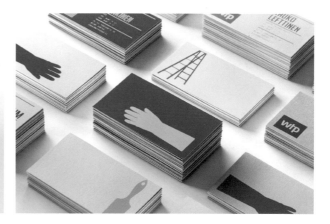

wtp

WALDO
TROMMLER
PAINTS

PL 53, PORVOONTIE
30, 01301 VANTAA
TEL 0207 75 26
FAX 0207 75 27
INFO@WTPGROUP.FI
WWW.WTPGROUP.FI

TAKE YOUR PLEASURES SERIOUSLY.

ART IS NOT WHAT YOU SEE

WALDO TROMMLER PAINTS

ALKYD PAINT

wtp

ULJAS LONNBOHM

KAUKO LEFTTINEN

ERKKI MAKINEN

HANNU POLVIANDER

ARVO SNELLMANN

ULJAS LONNBOHM

WALDO
TROMMLER
PAINTS

PL 53, PORVOONTIE
30, 01301 VANTAA
TEL 0207 75 26
FAX 0207 75 27

INFO@WTPGROUP.FI
WWW.WTPGROUP.FI

wtp

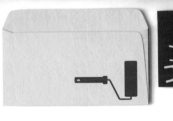

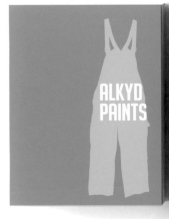

ALKYD PAINTS

IF YOU CAN PAINT ONE THING, YOU CAN PAINT EVERTHING

wtp

CREATIVITY IS THE DRUG I CANNOT LIVE WITHOUT

WATER
BURN
PAINTS

WHLL
TROM
PAINT

BASE

FLOOR

FACADE

WALDO
TROMMLER
PAINTS

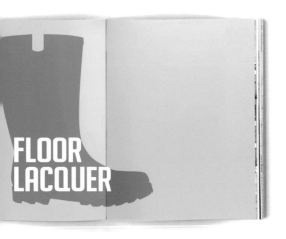

FLOOR
LACQUER

wtp

St Kilda Film Festival

Taking a digital evening twilight palette as the base, the Melbourne film festival campaign illuminated diversity, originality and artistic endeavour in domestic and foreign short films. The abstract colour was contrasted by an organic, geometric graphics on posters and programme.

Studio Brave
Client: City of Port Phillip

"Colour is an incredible tool because it can exist everywhere."

The Hope Slide

Described as "perseverance triumphing over adverse circumstances", the theme of The Hope Slide's namesake album is translated into an outburst of colour against a field of dull grey. The duo's name picks up a vibrant shade as the vinyl pocket slides into the die-cut sleeve with snipped corners.

Post Projects
Client: The Hope Slide

GF Smith

Without the restrictions posed by plates on lithographic machines, 'variable imaging' is one of the most exciting qualities offered by digital print. The package promotes GF Smith's digital paper and press in 10,000 unique illustrations, co-designed with digital artists at FIELD.

SEA

Illustration: FIELD
Client: GF Smith

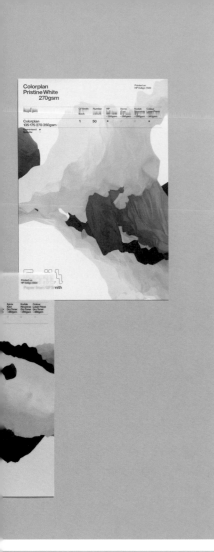

Pollen

Unfolded as a visual experimentation with vector illustrations and
paint, Pollen was originally an abstract cover art on squatting and
urban planning in Norway. The illustration is later produced as limited
gicleé print using pigment ink on fine art paper.

Grandpeople
Client: Eriksen & Skajaa

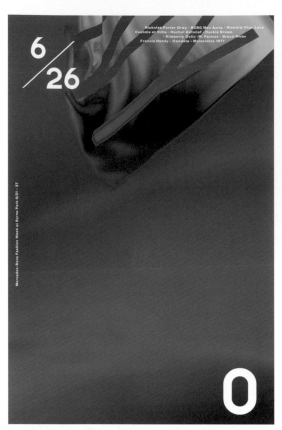

Nicholas Porter Grey · BCBG Max Azria · Richard Chai: Love
Cushnie et Ochs · Rachel Antonof · Duckie Brown
· Kimberly Ovitz ·M. Patmos · Bruce Webe
Francis Hendy · Candela · Maisonette 1977

6/26

O

Mercedes-Benz Fashion Week at Byrne Park 6/21 – 27

Nicholas Porter Grey · BCBG Max Azria · Richard Chai: Love
Cushnie et Ochs · Rachel Antonof · Duckie Brown
· Kimberly Ovitz ·M. Patmos · Bruce Webe
Francis Hendy · Candela · Maisonette 1977

6/25

I

Mercedes-Benz Fashion Week at Byrne Park 6/21 – 27

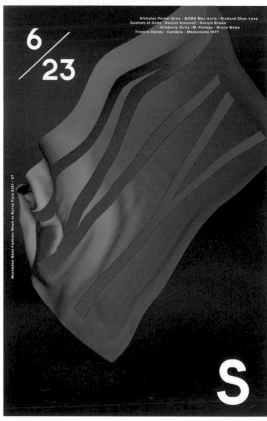

6/23

S

Mercedes-Benz Fashion Week at Byrne Park 6/21 – 27

Nicholas Porter Grey · BCBG Max Azria · Richard Chai: Love
Cushnie et Ochs · Rachel Antonof · Duckie Brown
· Kimberly Ovitz ·M. Patmos · Bruce Webe
Francis Hendy · Candela · Maisonette 1977

6/27

N

Mercedes-Benz Fashion Week at Byrne Park 6/21 – 27

6/24

Mercedes-Benz Fashion Week at Byrne Park 6/21 – 27

NY FASHION WEEK

NY Fashion Week has always been an event of glamorous extrava-
ganza. While fashion comes and goes, the swaying scarfs illustrated
variety in the field. The seven posters assembling the word F-A-S-H-
I-O-N count the week as an event calendar.

Paul Sangwoo Kim

Client: Art Center College of Design
Special credits: Clive Piercy

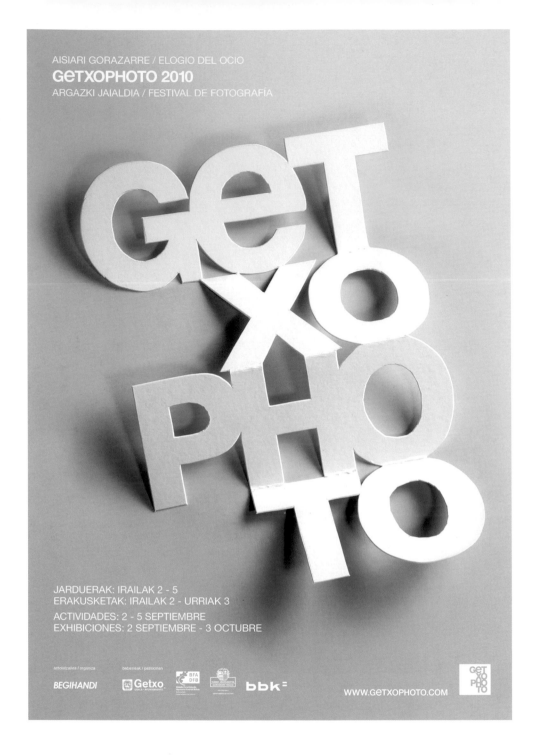

Getxophoto 2010

Taking the photo festival's logo as the centerpiece by tradition, the poster illustrated "leisure", its theme for 2010 as a festive paper chain picked out with colour lights. The festival was curated by Frank Kalero and took place in Getxo, Basque Country.

IS Creative Studio.

Photo: Alain Egues
Client: Getxophoto

Symbiosis

Symbiosis is part of the *Not For Commercial Use: Paste* series, containing five unbranded limited edition posters made to be posted anonymously around London. *NFCU: Paste* was a collaboration between Build and Generation Press which started life as a discussion about designer-printer relationship.

Build, Generation Press

H.A.Z.E Tonal Adventure

To Podhajsky, Colour is a dynamic interplay of darkness and light. Beneath the minimal artwork and subtle tonal shift presents Podhajsky's arguments about the universe and the idea that we are all gods of our own.

Leif Podhajsky

6人6色──みんなで集まるときの色

JC Crocker Pep

As a denim sub-label to JC, one of Sweden's leading fashion retailers, Crocker Pep's graphic language visualises the brand's multicoloured product range in an abstract sense. On top of that, the colours also dramatise the position and image of the brand.

Kurppa Hosk
Client: Jeans Company (JC)

Crocker
Pep!

"If relevant, colour is a key ingredient to revitalise and dramatise. In this project colour is a key element to interpret the colourful products."

images3   Karine Rochat

PHOTOLITHO
RETOUCHE
PRÉPRESSE

Images 3 SA
Avenue de France 23bis
Case postale
CH-1000 Lausanne 7
T +41 21 621 89 80
M +41 79 438 61 45
karine@images3.ch
www.images3.ch

images3   Denis Hauswirth

PHOTOLITHO
RETOUCHE
PRÉPRESSE

Images 3 SA
Avenue de France 23bis
Case postale
CH-1000 Lausanne 7
T +41 21 621 89 89
M +41 79 438 61 45
denis@images3.ch
www.images3.ch

images3   Matthieu Csakodi

PHOTOLITHO
RETOUCHE
PRÉPRESSE

Images 3 SA
Avenue de France 23bis
Case postale
CH-1000 Lausanne 7
T +41 21 621 89 89
M +41 79 438 61 45
matthieu@images3.ch
www.images3.ch

images3   Natalie Bossy

PHOTOLITHO
RETOUCHE
PRÉPRESSE

Images 3 SA
Avenue de France 23bis
Case postale
CH-1000 Lausanne 7
T +41 21 621 89 89
M +41 79 438 61 45
nathalie@images3.ch
www.images3.ch

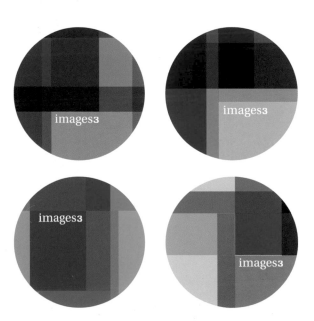

Images 3

Images 3 is a retouching, prepress and
lithography printery. The identity was conceived as an artistic interpretation of an
image's heart with colourful grids as pixels.

ENZED
Client: Images 3

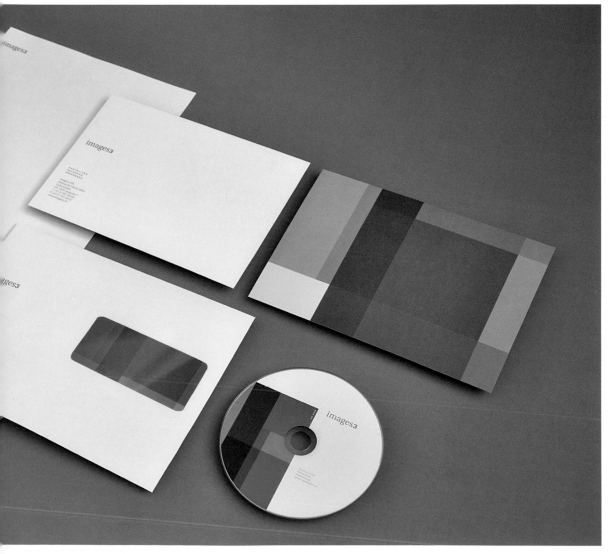

Film Commission Chile

Established to facilite movie production in Chile, Film Commission Chile has its
identity led by the industry's popular tool – duct tapes. Because of its flexibility,
the line and form of tapes as well recall the classic movie celluloid film.

Hey

Creative direction: Cristian Jofre
Photo: Roc Canals
Client: Film Commission Chile

103

Sonorama

Sonorama is the marriage of sound and panorama, the new soundscape. In connection with the venue, Helmo created a modular, tricoloured font accompanied with lively rhythms and the landscape of Besançon. The series contained four versions with different level of "noise" in the visual sense.

Helmo, Alice Guillier
Client: Sonorama Festival

BESANÇON
PAYSAGE
SONORE

INSTALLATIONS ET PARCOURS SONORES,
CONCERTS, FILMS MUSICAUX,
PERFORMANCES, SPECTACLES DE RUE...

8-11 OCTOBRE

WWW.SONORAMA-BESANÇON.COM

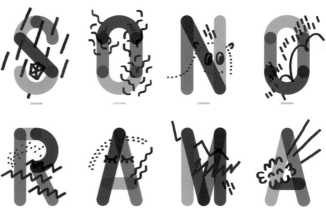

Colour Wheel Print / Notecards

A nostalgic print and notecard collection initiated to revoke the joy
of looking at old-time colour wheels now integrated with vector draw-
ings. The geometric versions was a fun alternative intended for the
sharing of love for colours with the world.

Present & Correct

Red
Rouge
Rojo
Rot
Rosso

Orange
Orange
Naranja
Farbe
Arancione

Yellow
Jaune
Amarillo
Gelb
Giallo

Green
Vert
Verde
Grün
Verde

Blue
Bleu
Azul
Blau
Azzurro

Purple
Violet
Morado
Lila
Porpora

BLO SWE TEA
OD AT RS

HON MOR DRA
OR AL MA

POW GOA CLA
ER LS SS

JES OWE SPE
SE NS ED

PEA TEA SPO
CE MS RT

London 2012 / Olympic Games

Out of disappointment in the official Olympic posters, Bræstrup created
a poster series himself, recounting what athletes had gone through during the games. The initial version saw "blood", "sweat" and "tears" resem-
bling the colours and arrangement of the Olympic rings.

Thomas Bræstrup

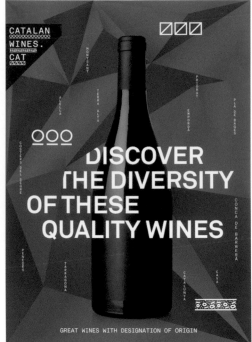

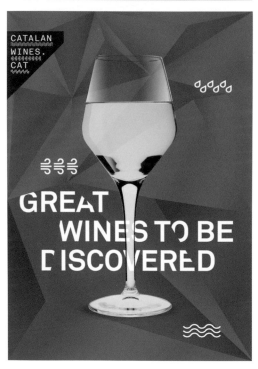

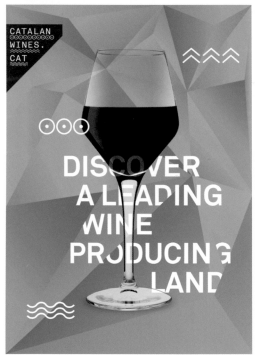

Catalan Wines

A collective wine branding strategy that targets both domestic and international wine lovers. From the logo to its variations, the communication system hints at the wine quality with a palette and graphic index, symbolic of the respective climatic conditions, geological structure and terrain of all wine regions in Catalonia.

Toormix

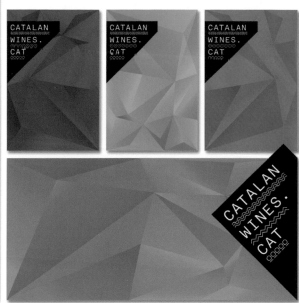

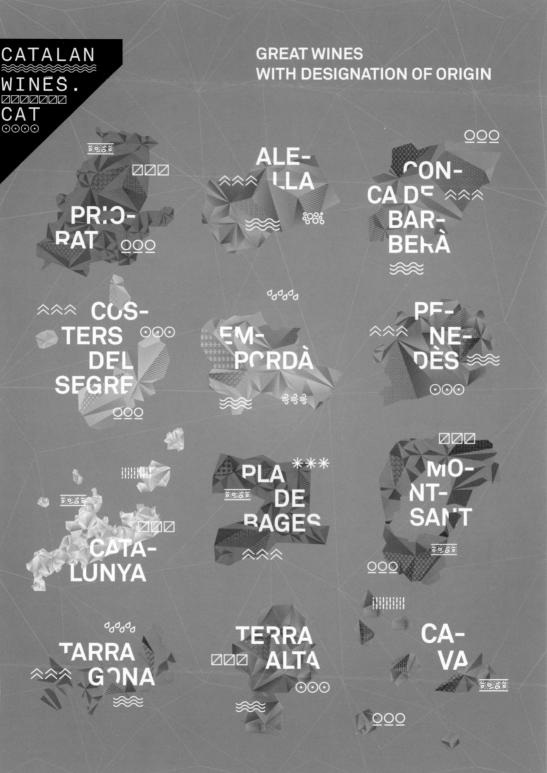

CATALAN
WINES.
CAT

GREAT WINES
WITH DESIGNATION OF ORIGIN

PRIO-RAT

ALE-LLA

CON-CA DE BAR-BERÀ

COS-TERS DEL SEGRE

EM-PORDÀ

PE-NE-DÈS

PLA DE BAGES

MO-NT-SANT

CATA-LUNYA

TARRA GONA

TERRA ALTA

CA-VA

Theatre CCCB

Theatre CCCB is a new addition to the Centre of Contemporary Culture in Barcelona. In response to the request for a typography-led approach, Hey accentuated the opening with a few exclamations of astonishment based on the entertainment business onomatopoeic expressions.

Hey

Photo: Roc Canals
Client: The Centre of Contemporary Culture in Barcelona (CCCB)

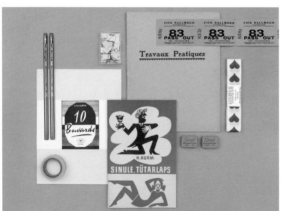

Colour Sets

Photography art set to collate vintage finds and an assortment
of office items sourced from different culture and countries
and unite them with hue. Visually the groups project a mix of
graphic shapes and packaging approaches.

Present & Correct

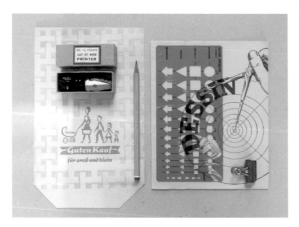

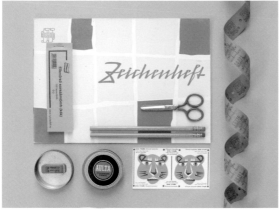

119

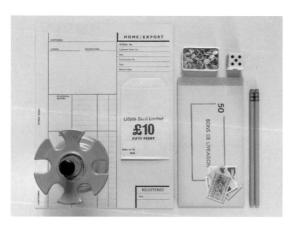

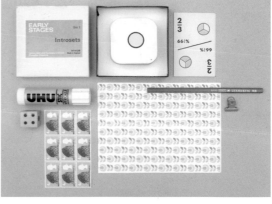

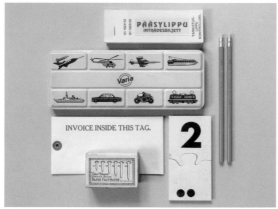

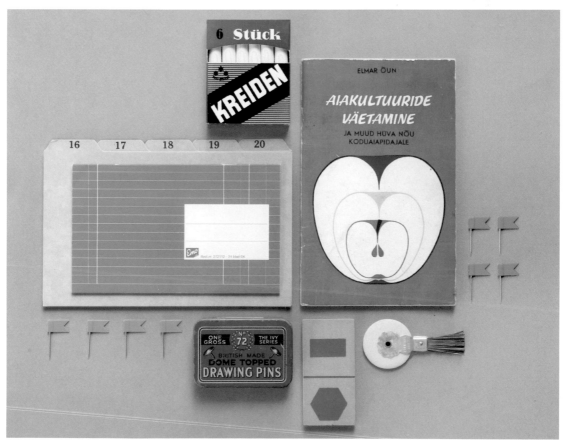

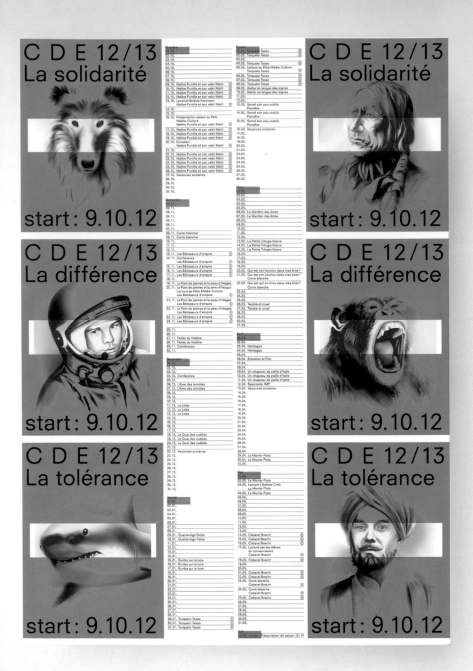

Comédie De l'Est 2012/2013

For the season 2012/2013, theatre La Comédie de l'Est is set to open itself for escapes and experience of tolerance, solidarity and difference in theatrical art. The programmes and posters are a budget solution to excite families in Colmar in the east of France.

Claudiabasel
Client: Comédie De l'Est

C D E 12 / 13
a différence

start : 9.10.12

C D E 12/13
La tolérance

start : 9.10.12

C D E 12/13
La solidarité

start : 9.10.12

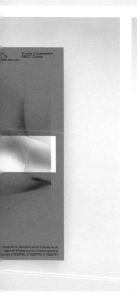

PechaKucha

With its origin in Japan, PechaKucha Night now also gathers young designers in Oslo to share thoughts and stories with 20 images in 20 seconds. Much attention was paid to the paper and formats to relate its root, while the white background ease reading in low light.

Your Friends
Client: Pecha Kucha Oslo

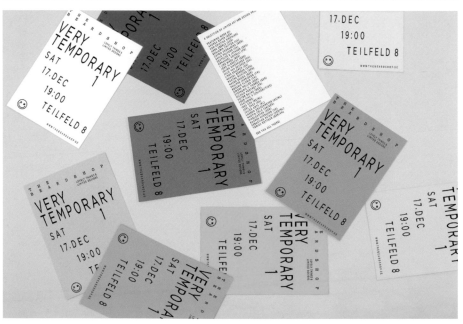

The Beardshop

The Beardshop is an online marketplace for limited edition design, art and fashion products. Through multicolour packaging and stationery, The Beardshop presents its products individually by colour based on Johannes Itten's colour theory.

I LIKE BIRDS

Website coding: Thomas Lempa
Client: The Beardshop

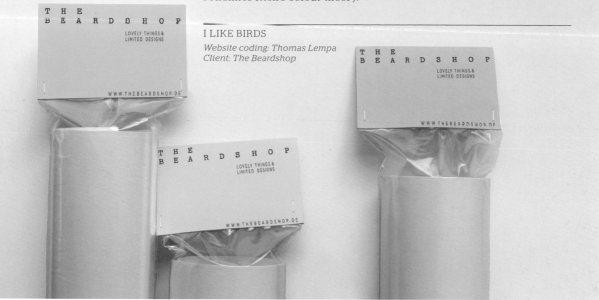

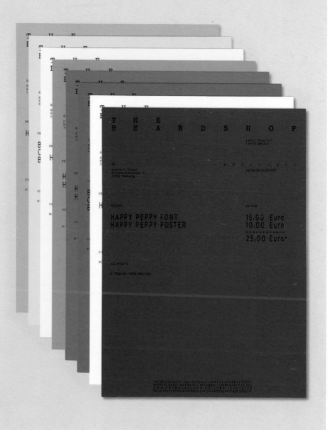

deep mat

deep mat is a Japanese paper available in colours suggestive of fine wine and everything related. To present the paper's printing potentials, deep mat sample kit plays up its weight and texture using only hot stamping and embossment in print.

artless Inc.
Client: Heiwa Paper Co.,Ltd.

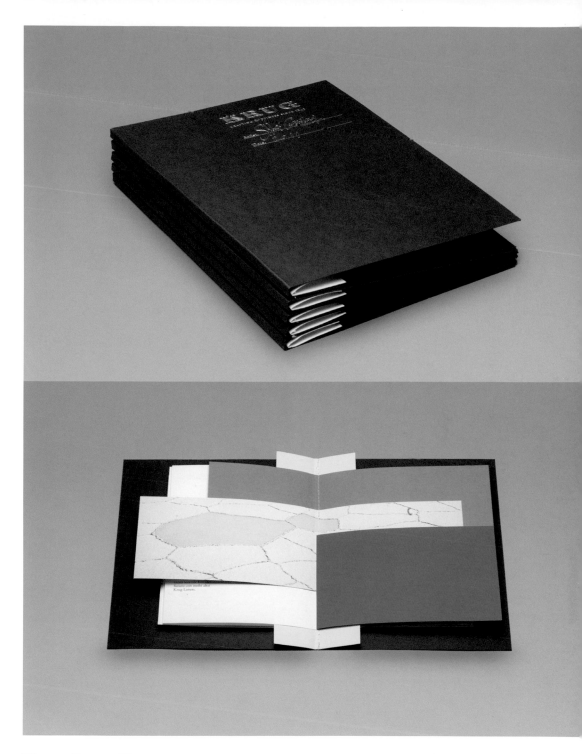

Krug Press Dossier

This press dossier presents a new "Krug lover", Dutch artist Scarlett Hooft Graaftland who shared Krug's artistic values in pursuing happiness and art. The booklet features a playful amaglam of paper and format to reflect the artist's unique approach to landscape photography.

Artworklove
Client: Champagnes Krug, Mademoiselle Noï

Get Lost….

Titled *Get Lost…*, the Fredrik Raddum retrospective contextualised the artist's work and development to coincide with his solo exhibition at ARoS, Denmark. The book was compiled based on a socialising process, divided by colour chapters for a structural study.

Your Friends

Artwork: Fredrik Raddum
Curation: Marie Nipper
Text: Theodor Barth
Photo: Einar Aslaksen
Client: Aarhus Museum of Modern Art (ARoS)

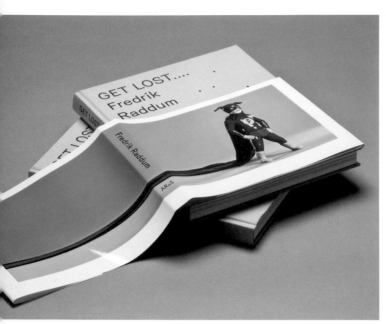

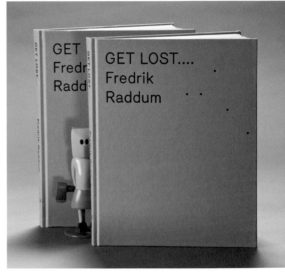

Urbanized

A set of four limited edition prints for Gary Hustwit's documentary 'Urbanized', the third and last documentary of his Design Trilogy. The pictograms depict the four themes from the film, namely housing, mobility, public space and infrastructure.

Build
Client: Plexi

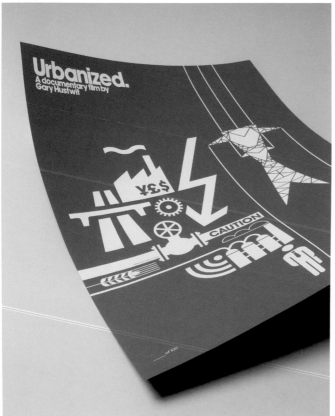

Visual Identity Proposal for ARoS

Embracing ARoS' vision and the museum's architectural concept inspired by "Divine Comedy", WAAITT™ proposed a logo that corresponds the three canticas and ARoS' three-storey structure with a stack of three in three colours. The proposal was not used.

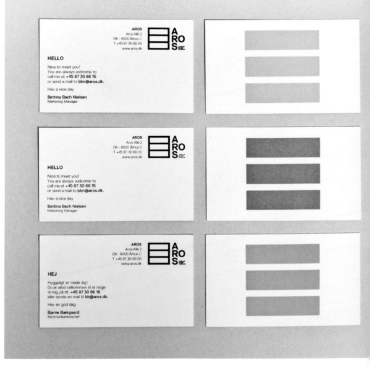

WAAITT™

Photo: ARoS, Nadav Kander (David Lynch portrait)
Client: Aarhus Museum of Modern Art (ARoS)

Gift Wrap

A simple gift wrapper design inclusive of printed ribbons in four colours.
For a humorous touch, all wrapping paper contains a factual description of
what is wrapped inside while the gift, however, remains a surprise.

Derek Kim
Client: Approved

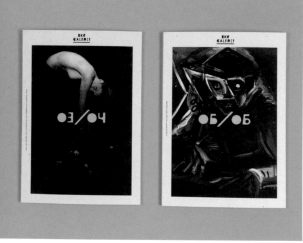

BKC Gallery

Silkscreen poster and leaflet design for BKC Gallery. Produced with single-colour printing, the bi-monthly newsletter updates visitors on the gallery's new programmes, as well as a new colour for a refreshing feel.

Anymade Studio
Client: BKC Gallery

The House of Art Brno

Brochure design for a series of exhibitions organised by The House of Art Brno. Each edition's cover features a unique design derived from the gallery's logo with no regular rules.

Anymade Studio

Client: The House of Art Brno

Fontsmith '10 Years in Type'

10 Years in Type celebrates Fontsmith's ten years of dedication to type design. Speaking directly to designers, the key users of Fontsmith's products, the box set recounts the ten best influences that Fontsmith fonts has brought to the world in the last decade.

Thompson Brand Partners
Client: Fontsmith

"It acts as an accent throughout the catalogue — a tinted background for the text listings."

There's espionage – a cloak-and-dagger novel in perhaps the most conspicuous publisher's binding I've ever seen — Short List 2

Prudishness is hidden in verse; a bookseller is eulogised and Marie-Antoinette is revealed in her own words. Literally — Short List 2

A Chechen jihadist, a Nantucket Quaker, and an amputee poet — Short List 3

Russians in London, American crime hits St Petersburg, and Soviet children read about their peers in New York — Short List 2

An Enlightenment guide to the art of reading, and a WWII saboteur's handbook disguised as a pocket dictionary — Short List 1

There's music – the first musical depiction of a train, and an eighteenth-century binder uses up an unwanted score — Short List 2

Thanks for buying these books, enjoy! Simon

Simon Beattie Catalogues & Stationery

Simon's identity is all about celebrating the eclectic nature of his antiquarian books. A good mix of classic types was adopted to depict his devotion to European language and culture, where vintage colours hold everything together under one identity.

Purpose
Client: Simon Beattie

Invisible Comics

To celebrate the crest of Serbian alternative comics scene from 1980s to 2010s, National Library of Serbia published "Invisible Comics" in three language indicated by colours. Studio Metaklinika was responsible for the publication's editing, art direction and design.

Metaklinika

Client: National Library of Serbia
Special credits: Johanna Marcade, Turbo Comix

THE
INVIS
IBLE
COM
ICS

NEVI
DLJI
VI
STR
IP

Predictions Series

Predictions is a calendar series that interprets fakery by placing relevant events outside their original context to confuse. Colour was a reference to the respective seasons and visual aids to tell the individual months apart.

Tim Wan

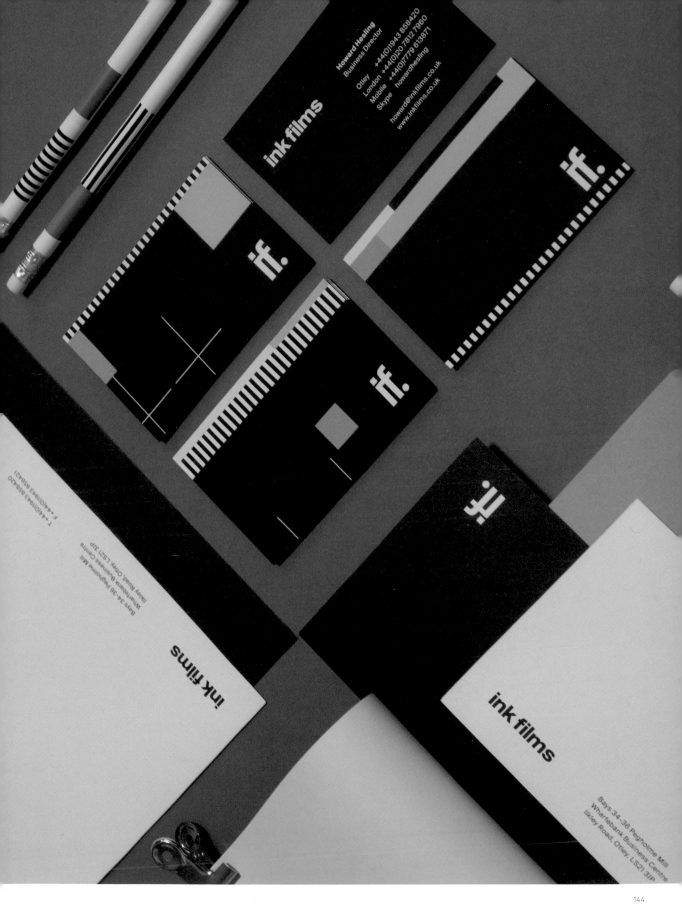

Ink Films Identity

Ink Films is a British production company officially established by a group of experienced directors in 2009. To strengthen its brand image despite its deceptively short history, implicit in the identity was the group's vast knowledge of the industry and film production conveyed in the minimal test patterns on the stationery's edge.

R.I.S. Projects
Client: Ink Films

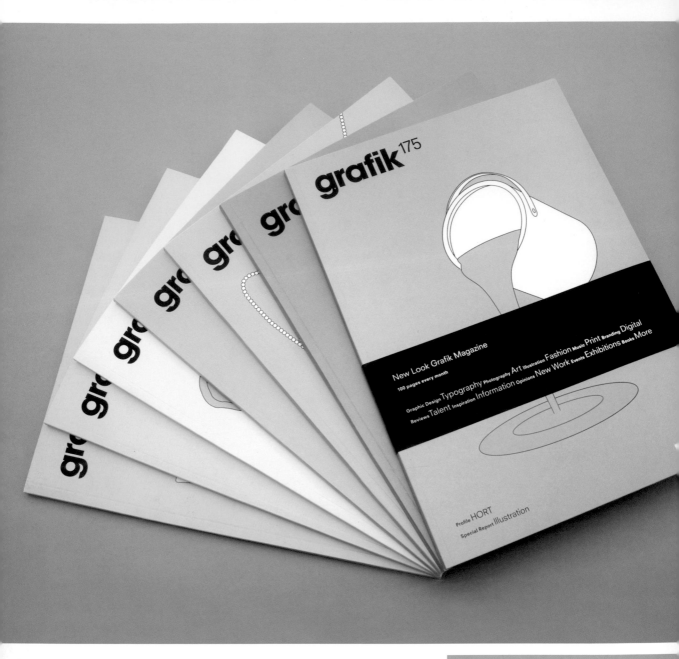

Grafik magazine issue 175—181

New cover approach devised using Caulfield-esque illustrations and a mid-range palette to establish a secondary brand language beside Grafik's brand name. Each illustration schematically reveals the cover story through one object for every month.

Matilda Saxow

Client: Grafik magazine

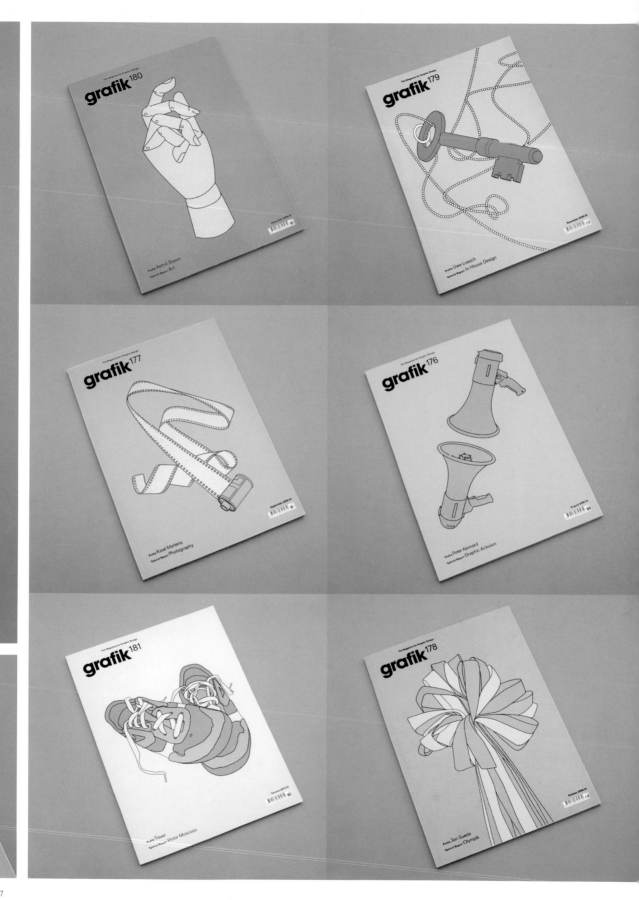

Kyoorius Designyatra 2011

The theme for Kyoorius Design Yatra 2011 was 'NEXT' with conversations swirling around analogue versus digital. Central to the conference's identity was ink rollers, convertible into installations and animations, with which attendants could easily interact.

Sueh Li Tan
Creative direction: Figtree Design
Client: Kyoorius

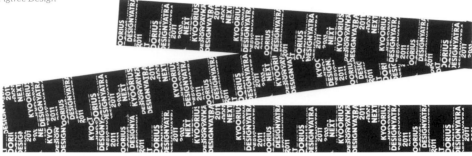

Formación Profesional

Photography for the promotion of professional training at vocational schools in Barcelona. A perfect blend of sensuality with the avant garde, the images invite the youth to acquire professional training as to distinguish themselves in the business world.

Paco Peregrín
*Agency: *S,C,P,F...*
Model: Nuria Plaza, Alexander Ardid (Sight Management)
Client: Barcelona City Council

"The use of colour in my photography is a product of my background in design, painting, theatre and my Mediterranean origins."

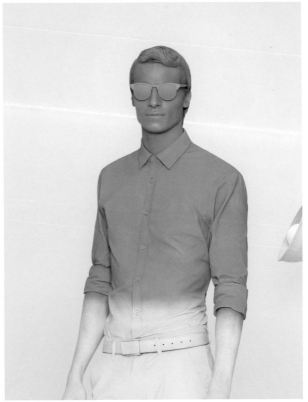

docomo Palette UI 2011

Lit up with jazzy projections created by WOW, the tunnel space highlighted 'docomo Palette UI' as a new user-friendly app management system at TOKYO DESIGNERS WEEK 2011. While moving images related the UI's dynamic interactions, the large screens allowed a total colour experience emphasised by the app.

TORAFU ARCHITECTS, WOW

Production: Taiyo Kogyo, DENTSU
Programming: RaNa design, WOW
Sound / Lighting: Prism
Sound source: WOW, Masato Hatanaka
Photo: WOW
Client: docomo

Nike Sportswear

Finished with 3D printing, the full-scale sci-fi sprinter celebrated the return of Nike Sportswear V-series to Stockholm as part of NSW ART RUN where art meets running. Captured at the middle of a good run, the athlete glowed with UV lights in the dark.

Igor Zimmermann

Manufacture: WEDO
Client: Nike Sportswear
Special credits: Andreas Olsson

COLORPLANE

Like neon kites twirling in the wind, 'whirls' underlies Midnight Rendez-Vous' 2012 S/S collection, COLORPLANE. Composed only of tops, the collection evokes the canvas of parachutes, hang-gliders and hot air balloons with its bright colours, graphic cuts and smooth materials.

Midnight Rendez-Vous
Graphic design : Alexandre Delo Rivière
Photo: Jules Faure

CHIMERA ～ CAVERN

Chimera Cavern

Part of Golden's thesis poster project on composing messages based around human needs and wants.

Chris Golden

"Colour helps me brainstorm and focus on what I want to communicate when developing a design."

CHIMERA 〰 CAVERN

Portfolio 2010

In a set of eight, each containing one project, Studio mw's portfolio laid emphasis on print, their favourite field and core of business. Each leaflet corresponded to a project in subject, with colours echoing the palette in shaded tones.

Studio mw

Malstatt Urban Art

Announcement for a Malstatt Urban Art exhibition where university students join forces on temporary interventions in public space. The invite was an abstract map showing the main streets, a railroad and river specific for the location where the performances took place.

Studio Laucke Siebein
Client: Bernardete Fernandes

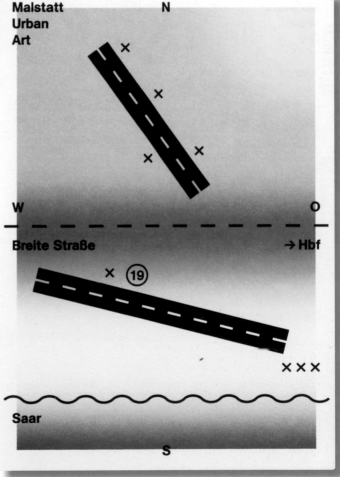

Jelly & Light

Set creation combining designer lamps and unusual
materials as the base. The block sculptures create a
new aesthetic chemistry between the lamps and the
jelly structure with colour gradations and edgy forms.

Le Creative Sweatshop

Photo: Fabrice Fouillet
Lighting: Nessimo by Artémide
Special credits: Artémide (Castore), Ionna Vautrin (Binic)

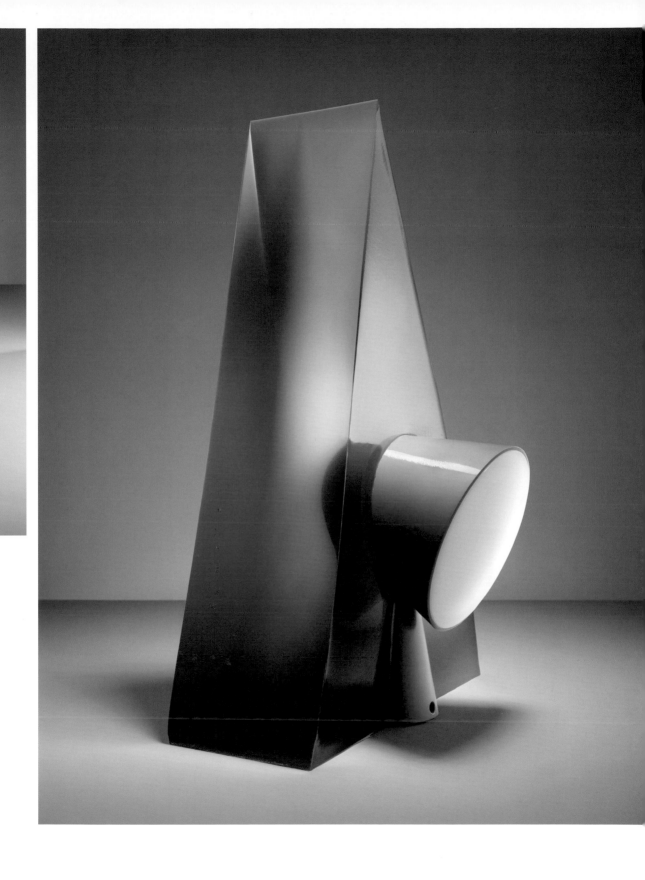

Mischlicht RGB

"Mischlicht RGB" can be briefly interpreted as "RGB mix light" forcing light to illuminate through acrylic glass tinted with additive primary and secondary colours besides white, as the sum of all. The lamp shade is matched with RGB cables which extend towards the ceiling.

macmeier, Fabian Nehne
Self-initiated at Appel Design Gallery Berlin

"The geometric approach and the colour variation of light make for a simplistic starting point for a design to tell a story."

TAPE FACE

Experimental lettering made from spaced-out masking tapes, so as to play on "type face" in a literal sense. If composed in Olympic colours, the letter will give you the Olympic rings without question.

Lo Siento

JAZZDOR

Following JAZZDOR's tradition of using portraits as the starting point, Helmo approached the posters for JAZZDOR Strasbourg and JAZZDOR Berlin with odd sounds and energy graphically emitting from the musicians. White smoke was photographed and digitally coloured for a magnetic effect.

Helmo

Photo: Christophe Urbain
Client: JAZZDOR

JAZZ

D OR

06 - 21

N OVE

23ᵉ
ÉDITION
–

-MBR E

200 9

TÉL
03 88 36 30 48
–

> STRAS-

BOUR G

–

–

WWW.JAZZDOR.COM

171

PIGMENTPOL® Identity

Recently liberated from the German Reproplan Group, PIGMENT-POL® operates three subsidiaries serving a client base from across the creative industry. The idea of individuality and possibilities is embedded in a varied yet coherent design derived from a hexagon, enabled by a generative software provided by FELD.

ATMO Designstudio & FELD | studio for digital crafts

Photo: Thomas Schlorke
Client: PIGMENTPOL®

"It is really important to come up with your own set of colour rules and always be willing to question them."

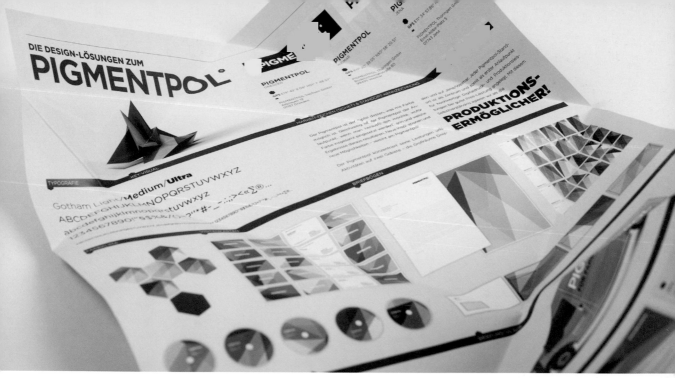

Pony Bar Monthly Programme

Monthly calendars for Pony Bar in Hamburg. Illustrations and the colour of each month go in tune with the season and what the bar has to offer at specific time. The result is an unconventional programme of cultural activities to look forward to.

La Tigre
Client: Pony Bar

"Colour helps seasons to reveal themselves slowly."

APRIL 2011

PONY BAR

MAI 2011

PONY BAR

JUNI 2011

PONY BAR

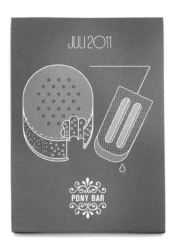

JULI 2011

PONY BAR

AUGUST 2011

PONY BAR

SEPTEMBER 2011

PONY BAR

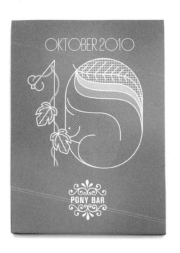

OKTOBER 2010

PONY BAR

NOVEMBER 2010

PONY BAR

DEZEMBER 2010

PONY BAR

Vicente Aleixandre Library Visual Identity & Signage System

Striking a fabulous contrast against the grey city of Badia del Vallès was one of Gràcia's tactic to draw the public to the renovated Vicente Aleixandre Library. Bold and transparent stripes let the space breathe in colour and natural light, while completing the update with vitality and a new look.

Txell Gràcia Design Studio
Client: Badia del Vallès City Council

Färg

Swedish for 'colour', Färg amasses the beauty of tints and hues from everyday life. Despite the minor differences in coloration when looked at individually, the general pictures offer an alternative gaze at life with regard to colour.

Kontor Kontur

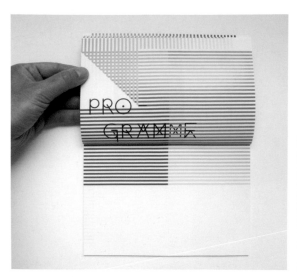

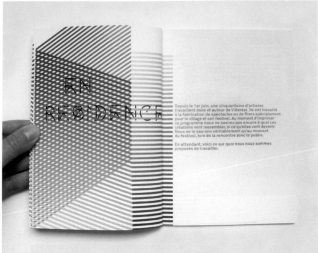

Un Festival à Villeréal 2011

With regard to the theatre festival's 2011 theme "Mythology origins", Ledowski referenced the origin of modern alphabets with phoenician-style types. Words intertwined with lines inspired by Geoffrey Boucher's string installations in town, as theatre plays prevail the village.

Wanja Ledowski
Architecture: Geoffroy Boucher
Client: Vous êtes ici

Gandules' 10

More than ever, Gandules 2010 was full of fiction, aimless characters, endless searches and journeys to the unknown. Titled *Lost, lost, lost*, the movie section of the cinema season was all about the desire for movements – getting out of a place, escape, change or conceive another world.

Hey
Photo: Roc Canals
Client: The Centre of Contemporary Culture in Barcelona (CCCB)

On Strike

"On Strike" is Ontour's 2011 autumn/winter collection inspired by activists, protests and underground resistance. Emotionally evocative yet implicit, the wordless multicoloured placards summarised all angry voices for free interpretation in the season's lookbook.

Raw Color
Client: Ontour

185

Eating by Design

"Eating by Design" explores all avenues of food design and its complicated relationship with man. Installed to give visitors a brief introduction to each exhibition room, each panel features a stencilled title, concept explanation and a special shade, like the pervasive supermarket signboards and print ads.

Raw Color
Curation: Marije Vogelzang, Koos Flinterman
Project management: Floor van Ast
Client: Premsela

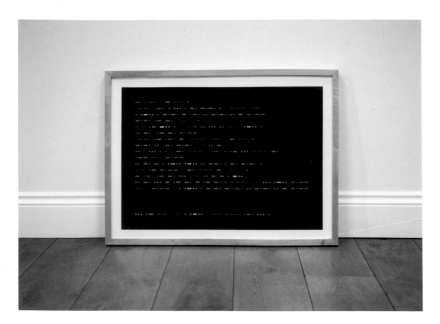

The Art of Code

As Samuel Morse said, 'If the presence of electricity can be made visible in any part of the circuit, I see no reason why intelligence may not be transmitted instantaneously by electricity'. While every alphabet was assigned a unique colour, Morse's words became visually intriguing in double codes.

Mad Keen Design & Art Direction
Photo: Archie Stephens

Visualising the London Underground

The London Underground is a wealth of statistics, figures, facts and history. In a much simplified language, the collection visualises the opening dates of the Underground lines, the overall lengths of the lines and the amount of Underground stations served by each line.

Mad Keen Design & Art Direction
Photo: Archie Stephens

Project 365, Information design

Project 365 graphically charted 365 daily top search news and events during 2009 acquired via Google Trends. Stackable pyramids were handfolded in five sizes, with one colour for each month, to materialise counts and categorise findings in chronological order.

Lemongraphic

HKU-Award

Asked for a poster set using the theme "superheroes" for HKU-Award 2010, Studio wilfredtimo imagined the nominees as abstract alter egos with a cartoony twist. As when superman bends metals, posters came complete with a metallic finish which then inspired the prize design.

Studio wilfredtimo
Client: Utrecht School of the Arts (HKU)

Beyond Risør

Beyond Risør is a biennial conferences with a focus on life-enhancing designs. Built on its slogan "light creates moods" for 2010, Bleed developed a visual system that could trace emotional words in followers' tweets. The result was a vibrant and real-time profile of the audience's response that varied consistently as shades.

Bleed
Client: Myspace

Lago Film Fest Visual Identity

Every year Lago Film Fest brings a global perspective on documentaries and short movies in a small village near Treviso, Italy. The 2010 festival related the event with one of the event's peculiarity, with neon projections suggesting the open-air screening on streets and outside the villagers' homes.

Studio Iknoki

Graphic design: Matteo Zago
Client: Lago Film Fest

De Industria

De Industria is a collective art show dedicated to the art-industry relationship. For its third edition, the poster metaphorically explored dexterity and ingenuity in the connection with interlocking matrix forms in a custom typeface.

Paolo Palma
Client: Comune di Fermignano

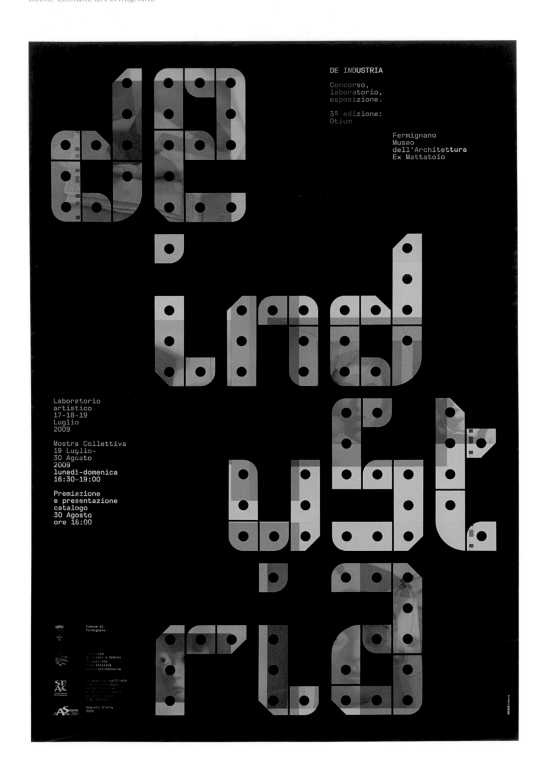

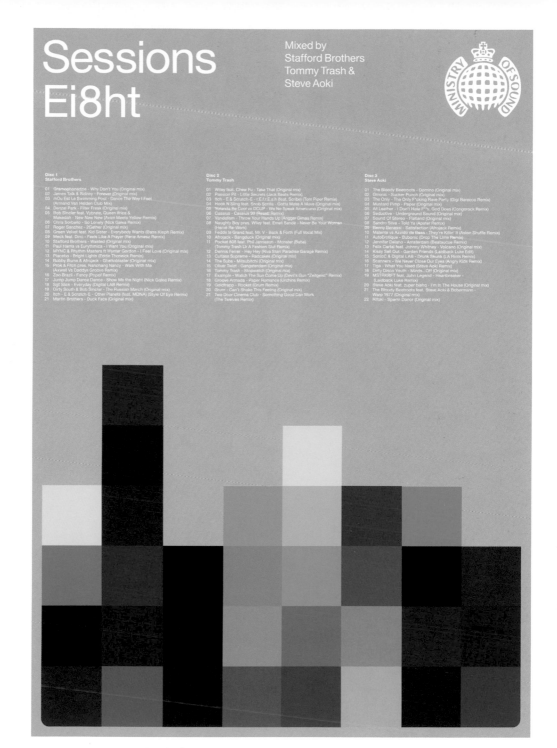

Ministry of Sound

Opened in 1991, Ministry of Sound was one of the key locations in the development of house music and super clubs in Britain in the early 90's. For its eighth session, the poster pictured rhythms in a burst of colours and stack of giant pixel cubes.

Holt

Client: Ministry of Sound

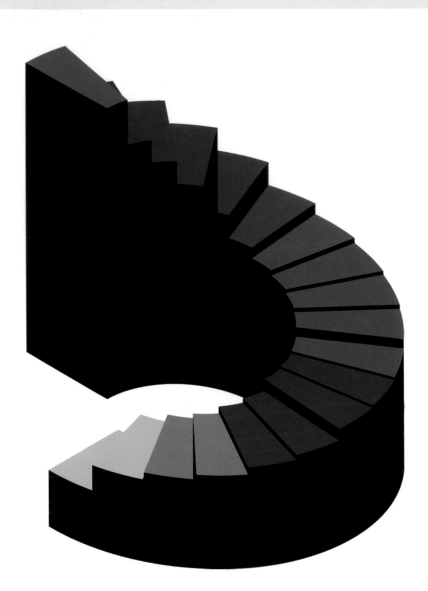

BOURGEOIS
Phase One.

A visual collaboration between
D. Crooks and D Kim.

Note: This poster contains an element from
an unused commisioned project.

Bourgeois

Deconstructed Modernism. Started as a commissioned work and ended up an artistic collaboration with Darhil Crooks from Esquire Magazine. Bourgeois is purely an exploratory piece for self expression and experimentation based on unused projects.

Derek Kim

Red Bull Music Academy presents
12 x 12 at The Scala

Red Bull Music Academy London

During the Red Bull Music Academy London held at The Scala, everything was composed around '12'. Here, the 12 vinyl records represented the dozen of 12-minute music sections performed by 12 heavyweight producers with a nod to the 12-inch records, for how it shaped modern music culture.

Bunch

Illustration: James Joyce
Client: Red Bull Music Academy

Supervision

Kerstin zu Pan's choice of rainbow-hue is a fitting metaphor since rainbows are not fully committed to our reality. *Supervision* is zu Pan's supersensory world captured by her camera, as well as our eyes and mind but never permanently in the dogmatic spaces of the body.

Kerstin zu Pan

Model: Britta Thie
Makeup: Karla Neff
Hair: Acacio da Silva
Project text: Ahmad Jordan

The Moment in A Springs

To Daisy Balloon, spring is about single moments coming together as a cycle. As colourful rubber bags or air-filled balloons, the wondrous assemblage of substance visualised new visions and celebrated 'transience' as well as the beauty of the moments in posters and window display.

Daisy Balloon

Photo: Hiroshi Manaka
Photo retouching: Yoshiaki Sakurai
Makeup: Ken Nakano
Hair: Koji Ichikawa
Styling: Koji Oyamada
Client: Osaka Takashimaya

Wear(e) the Future

At present, the future means approach-
ing "the end of world" in many people's
mind. FRAC Nord-Pas-de-Calais however
sees a different side. "Wear(e) the Future"
is an exhibition of artists' vision for the
teenagers of 2030. The poster calls up an
abstract but delightful mix of things that
we often overlooked.

Zim&Zou
Client: FRAC Nord Pas-de-Calais

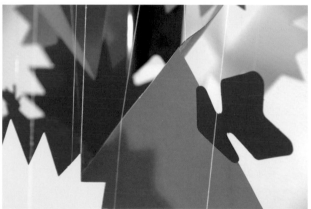

Bank of America
Market Data Mirrors

Integrated into the architecture of the Bank of America Tower, Market Data Mirrors display live, animated data feeds on a mirrored wall at the trade floor elevator bank. Data sets are differentiated into a variety of colourful patterns and shapes to convey values, volume and trends.

Second Story Interactive Studios
AV integration: Three Byte Intermedia, Excel Media
Environment design: C2 Creative
Client: C2 Creative for Bank of America

Building for the 2000 — Watt Society: The State of Affairs

Inspired by thermograms, Raffinerie devised and erected a nine-metre "energy mountain" in gradated colours to exemplify "sustainable building" as a key ecological solution. The exhibition was created in cooperation with Holzer Kobler Architekturen.

Raffinerie AG für Gestaltung

Client: City of Zurich
Special credits: Holzer Kobler Architekturen

Accidental Archives

Beginning as a means of sorting through the artist's massive collection of images and objects, *Accidental Archives* came as a record of experience with a different story to tell in every resulting pictures. The colour theme was conceived as visually the most immediate means of categorisation on site.

Sara Cwynar

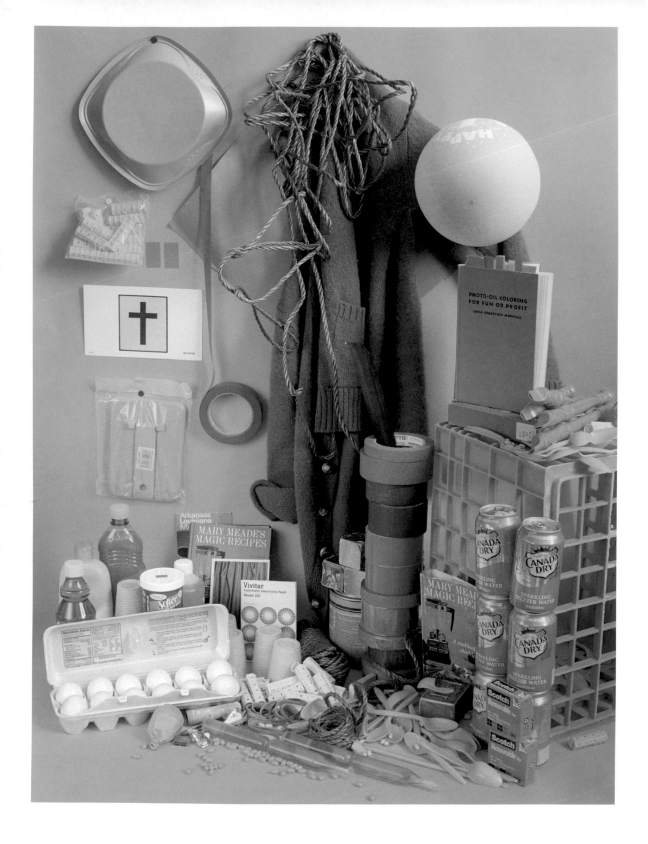

DreamBox

With RGB wallpaper, Carnovsky explored both the real and the fantastic, the true and the verisimilar in the way medieval bestiaries did. With a catalogue of natural motifs in three colour layers, RGB presented the antique theme of the metamorphosis as an unceasing transformation of shapes from a "primigenial chaos".

carnovsky
Client: Elisabeth Leriche

"Colour is the ground base of our work. From all possible point of views — scientific, aesthetic, physiologic — it is either the medium or the message of our work."

La Selva - RGB
The Black Series

Specially created for the duo's solo show, La Selva took advantage of the exhibition space and explored "jungle" in a juxtaposition of dense vegetation and bizarre creatures against the dark. Erected in three overlapping layers of red, green and blue, the jungle unveiled its infinities under filters in respective colours.

carnovsky

Photo: Jeff Metal
Client: Jaguarshoes Collective

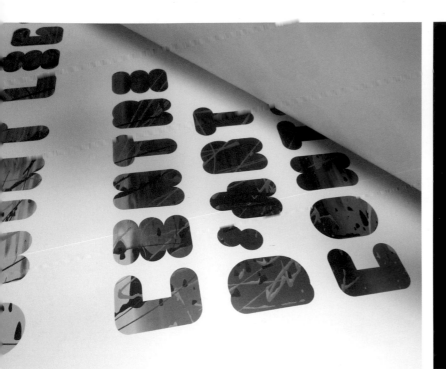

Parc Saint Léger, Centre d'art contemporain

The graphic identity of Parc Saint Léger, Centre d'art contemporain is a coherent, scalable system of round letters and marks which one can climb in real life and comprehend in print. The system also extends to the signage and banners designs of the recreational space.

Fanette Mellier

Photo: Jeff Metal
Client: Parc Saint Léger, Centre d'art contemporain

Theater St.Gallen

Subject to a strict grid and silkscreened in duo colours, the monthly posters, print ads and programmes for Theater St.Gallen allowed for individualities for separate events at nominal cost. Typographic effect were intended to be reinforced through the selective use of colour, production details and special inks.

Bureau Collective
Client: Konzert und Theater St.Gallen

224

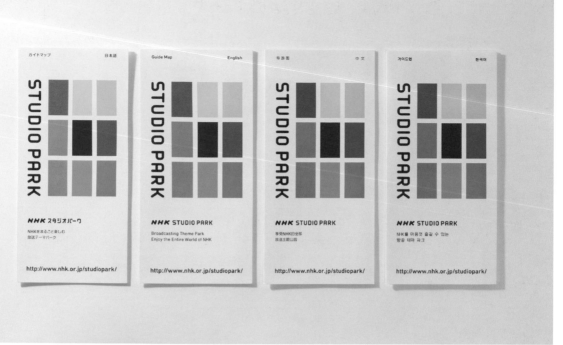

NHK Studio Park

NHK Studio Park targets a broad audience of different age and background, whoever wishes to experience broadcasting in Japan. NHK Studio Park's logo can be identified as nine 16:9 TV screens, with colours suggestive of televised images, activity zones and hospitality in space.

ujidesign

Direction: NHK Enterprise Inc.
Architecture: Takashi Nakahara, Tsuyoshi Tanio
Photo: ©NHK
Client: Japan Broadcasting Corporation (NHK)

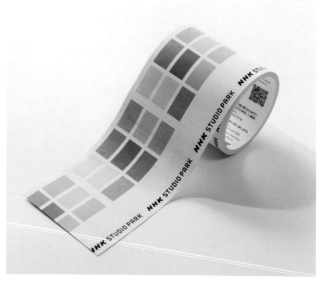

The Gourmet Tea

Being the first teahouse of The Gourmet Tea, the architectural design was conceived as an economic solution to rapidly transform the long, narrow room into a concept store. The palette is an exposition of the brand's 35 tea blends in total, each assigned a colour to tell the formulas apart.

Alan Chu, Cristiano Kato
Photo: Djan Chu
Client: The Gourmet Tea

The Gourmet Tea — Cidade Jardim

The third store of The Gourmet Tea inherits the brand's colour approach on its earlier teahouses but with more tactics to fully utilise space. Like an ordinary multi-coloured box when closed, the shop unveils its name, a cashier and a joyful array of racks from the hatch as it opens business at a São Paulo shopping centre.

Alan Chu

Team: Thiago Moretti
Photo: Djan Chu
Client: The Gourmet Tea

72DP

72DP is an immersive mural conceived to breathe life into the concrete underground carpark with little inlet of natural light. Like a winding ribbon, the resulting installation is a dynamic mix of overlapping geometric forms that respond to the angularity of the architecture designed by Marsh Cashman Koolloos.

Craig & Karl

Photo: Katherine Lu
Client: Private commission

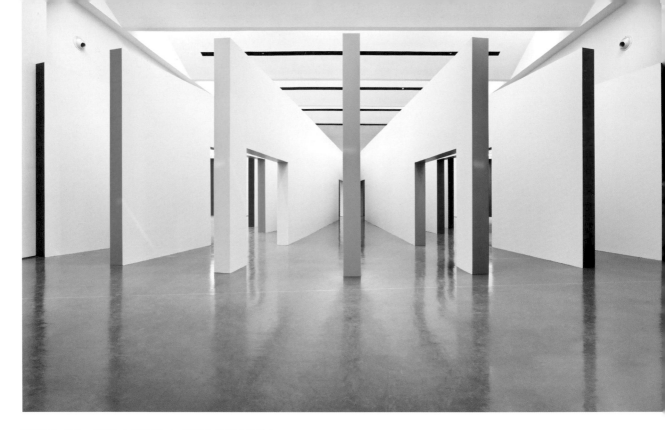

TDM5: GRAFICA ITALIANA

Exhibition design for Triennale Design Museum, imagining the space as a blank book to support exhibition materials spanning books, letters, advertising, video and signposting. The rainbow labyrinth was said to connect Heaven and Earth presented in the event.

Fabio Novembre, Dino Cicchetti,
Patrizio Mozzicafreddo, Giorgio Terraneo
Graphic design: Leftloft / Photo: Pasquale Formisano
Client: Triennale di Milano

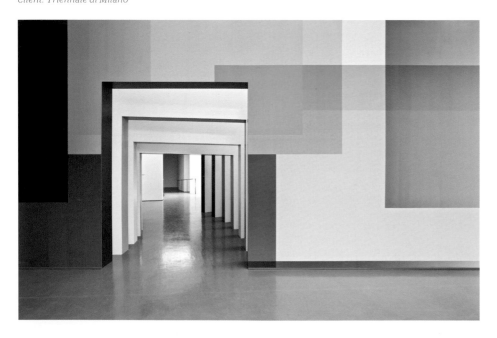

The Rainbow Thieves

The Rainbow Thieves was an epic collection of 40 Nemo Chairs, each soaked in a unique colour after their devious attempt to steal rainbow, inspired by *One Thousand and One Nights*. The exhibition was part of "Design Superheroes" for Moscow Design Week 2010.

Fabio Novembre, Dino Cicchetti, Giuseppe Modeo

Production: Driade
Photo: Pasquale Formisano
Client: ARTCOM Media Group

Art Inflatable and Ephemeral

A massive environmental installation, giving space a new identity with colour and a simplified atmosphere as giant balloons mask the room. The concept works on the relation between the full and the empty, generating a dialogue with the space visitors go past.

Penique productions

Special credits:
Bathroom, Absolute Art Space Gallery (Sala Buit), CutOutFest 2011 (El Claustro); (in next spread) Market Estate Project 2010 (18 Clocktower Place), CSA La Tabacalera (El Sótano de la Tabacalera), Sense titol 2010 (Forat de l'escala), Choko Ho'ol Short-film (Choko Ho'ol)

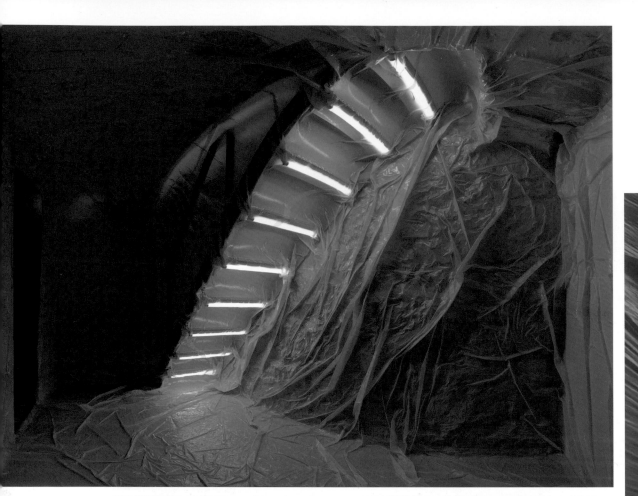

Sugamo Shinkin Bank / Shimura branch

To welcome visitors with a palpable sense of nature, Moureaux transformed the bank's façade into a rainbow mille-feuille. At night, the layers are illuminated, varying in degree responsive to seasons and time of day.

Emmanuelle Moureaux Architecture + Design

Photo: Nacasa & Partners Inc.
Client: Sugamo Shinkin Bank

École Maternelle Pajol

Intended for a wonderland for learning, the project involved custom design from furniture to the exterior space. While the front courtyard conveys urban optimistic signal, the interior space evokes emotions in plentiful colours and geometry with materials that are pleasant to touch.

Palatre et Leclere Architectes

Typography: Cyril Brejon
Photo : Luc Boegly
Client: City of Paris, Etoile Cinema, Ministry of Justice

Biography

Anagrama

Specialised in brand development and positioning, Anagrama's services reach the entire branding spectrum from strategic consulting to logotype, peripherals and captivating illustration design. The team is also expertised in the design and development of objects, spaces and multimedia projects.

P. 046-049

Andersen, Torsten Lindsø

A student at The Royal Danish Academy of Fine Arts working in all fields of media within branding and visual communication with a passion in typography.

P. 042-043

Anymade Studio

Founded in 2007 in the Czech Republic, the studio has evolved into a multifunctional platform for graphic design, photography, typography, illustration, video, motion design and sound. The team includes Petr Cabalka, Filip Nerad and Jan Šrámek aka VJ Kolouch.

P. 136-137

Aoki

Founded by Helena Svärd and Camilla Blomgren in 2009, the design and communication agency mainly works in the field of fashion and culture developing and packaging brands that they believe in, from identity to campaigns.

P. 012-013

artless Inc.

Establised in 2000 by Shun Kawakami, the interdisciplinary design and consulting firm works across all media including brand design, visual and corporate identity, advertising, packaging, product, video and motion graphics etc. The studio has won several prestigious international awards including CANNES Gold Lions, NY ADC, D&AD and The London International Award.

P. 128-129

Artworklove

Composed of Caroline de Vries, Marion Laurens and Ben Reece who founded the studio in 2009, Artworklove creates original identities, prints and digital materials for clients in the fields of arts and culture, luxury, moving image and publishing in Paris.

P. 130-131

Ascend Studio

An independent branding and design agency based in central London with a methodical approach of research, positioning, strategy and graphic communication.

P. 064

Ataz, Andrea

Graduated in graphic design in Murcia, Spain, Ataz received the Leonardo da Vinci scholarship for doing an internship in Belgium. Working both as a freelancer and an employee throughout the years, her work has been published in important annual publications in graphic design such as Select K and Selected B.

P. 032-033

Atipus

Barcelona-based graphic communication studio specialised in corporate identity, art direction, packaging design, editorial and web services, Atipus has been continually awarded by national and European design honours including the Laus Awards, ADC*E Awards and Anuaria.

P. 036-037

ATMO Designstudio & FELD | studio for digital crafts

ATMO and FELD leverage the relentless, precise and high-speed computational processes or custom machines to unfold works, while having the teams always at the helm which result in thought provoking, aesthetic and elegant works.

P. 172-175

Base Design

"Specialise in not specialising". With offices in Barcelona, Brussels, Madrid, New York, Santiago, and Chile, the agency works mainly in graphic design, art direction, audiovisuals, copywriting and typeface design for clients ranging from fashion houses to museums, educational institutions, and international corporations.

P. 018-021

Bleed

Based in Oslo, Norway and Vienna, Austria, the multidisciplinary design consultancy creates identity and experience through concept development, art direction, graphic design and service design, challenging today's conventions around art, visual language, media and identity.

P. 194

Blok Design

Specialising in brand identities and experiences, packaging, exhibit design, installations and editorial design, the studio also develops their own projects, including designing and publishing books and producing products that blend cultural awareness, the love of art and humanity to advance society and business alike.

P. 052

boymeetsgirl

Located in Berlin, Germany, the sustainable, multidisciplinary design studio is founded in 2011 making brands visible, ideas tangible, whether printed or digital, in space or on paper.

P. 024

Bræstrup, Thomas

Currently studying at the Royal Danish Academy of Fine Arts, Bræstrup designs posters, visual identities, publications, websites, and packaging with a passion for typography and a simple and rather conceptual approach.

P. 110-111

Brighten the Corners

Known for its simple but concept driven design, the team has worked for clients like the Goethe-Insitut, the British Council, the Department for Education, Accenture, Laurence King Publishing, Zumtobel Group and lately quite a lot with artist Anish Kapoor, happily switching between public sector, corporate and cultural environments.

P. 016

Browns

Since its inception in 1998, the studio has been producing sensitive work with a purity of form. The team works with many esteemed clients from around the world and have received numerous notable awards, most recently the Creative Review magazine's 'Design Studio of the Year 2011'.

P. 008-009

Build

Founded in 2001, the London-based graphic design consultancy focuses on design, art direction and identity with a specialty in high-end print for clients big and small. Both Build, as a studio, and Michael C. Place, the husband-&-wife founder, as a solo artist, have shown works in several exhibitions in the UK and abroad, including Tokyo, Paris, New York and London.

P. 095, 133

Bunch

A leading London-based design studio specialising in identity, literature, editorial, digital and motion, Bunch has been working with the world class brands like BBC, Nike, Diesel, Sony, Sky, and Red Bull for decades.

P. 199

Bureau Collective

A design studio founded in 2009 by Ollie Schaich and Ruedi Zürcher in St.Gallen, Switzerland working in different fields of graphic design.

P. 222-225

carnovsky

A Milan based artist/designer duo comprised of Francesco Rugi and Silvia Quintanilla.

P. 216-219

Chu, Alan

The Brazilian architect once had a studio with Cristiano Kato in São Paulo from 2004 to 2010. He is now a member of the Isay Weinfeld's creative team.

P. 230-233

Claudiabasel

Based in Basel, Switzerland, the studio works not only for clients but also teaches at local institutions like Visual Communication Institute, The Basel School of Design as well as schools abroad like Staatliche Hochschule für Gestaltung Karlsruhe in Germany.

P. 044-045, 122-123

Craig & Karl

Signature in the colourful, geometric pattern face, Craig Redman and Karl Maier work on projects in various medium including murals, sculpture, illustration, installation, interface design, typography, iconography, fabric patterns and print. They have exhibited internationally in many countries, most notably at the Musé de la Publicité, Louvre.

P. 234-235

Cwynar, Sara

Studied graphic design and photography at York University, the Canadian artist and graphic designer works mainly in photography, installation, and book-making. Represented by Cooper Cole Gallery, Cwynar has exhibited worldwide such as the Museum of Modern Art in New York and the Butcher Gallery in Toronto. Her work has been featured in numerous magazines like The New York Times Magazine and Beautiful Decay. She is one of Print Magazine's 20 Under 30 New Visual Artists for 2011.

P. 212-215

Daikoku Design Institute

Founded in 2011 by Daigo Daikoku working on projects from two- and three-dimensional to video and space design. Graduated in visual communication at Kanazawa College of Art in 2003, the designer has won numerous awards including the Tokyo ADC Prize and the D&AD Yellow Pencil Awards.

P. 040-041

Daisy Balloon

The collaboration between balloon artist Rie Hosokai and art director and graphic designer Takashi Kawada who were both born in 1976.

P. 204-205

Dalmau, Alex

Based in Barcelona, the art director specialises in graphic design, branding and corporate identity. After graduating from the Image and Design School (IDEP), he worked at various advertising agencies and design studios like Animal-BCN and Larsson-Duprez, and began working as a freelance in 2011. His clients include Mandarin Oriental Barcelona, Carolina Herrera, Adidas, etc.

P. 066-067

Emmanuelle Moureaux Architecture + Design

The French architect and designer residing in Tokyo since 1996 and founded the studio in 2003. Known for her technique handling colours as space makers, and for her unique colour scheming for architecture, interior, furniture and products, Moureaux is also an associate professor at the Tohoku University of Art & Design since 2008.

P. 246-247

ENZED

Based in Lausanne, Switzerland, the design consultancy specialises in prints, corporate identity, cultural and editorial design with a passion for typography and minimal Swiss design. Founded in 2001 by Nicolas Zentner, it is now a team of 3 including Mélanie Zentner and Mathieu Moret.

P. 100-101

Finch, Jonathan

Works mainly on identity, promotion and publication, Finch enjoys designing simple aesthetics that are carefully considered and well executed.

P. 068

FRVR

A small multidisciplinary graphic studio located in Prague, Czech Republic, specialising in brand creation and visual identities, custom typography, iconography, and character design with their approach rooted in strict, simple and rational graphic design style of 1960s and 70s.

P. 025

Golden, Chris

The multidisciplinary designer from the United States utilises illustration, collage and mixed media to create contextual pieces ranging from print, digital as well as motion projects besides a variety of side projects including djing and mixing music.

P. 162-163

Grandpeople

Located in Bergen and Drammen in Norway, the multidisciplinary design studio established by Christian Bergheim, Magnus Voll Mathiassen and Magnus Helgesen in 2005 offers services in graphic design, art direction and illustration for clients from different fields like Nike, Converse, Microsoft, Grafik Magazine, Tokion, Escalator records, etc.

P. 090-091

Happy F&B

Established in Gothenburg in 1997 as a part of the Forsman & Bodenfors group expertised in branding and communication, Happy F&B creates and develops brands from entire corporate identities and packaging lines to complex single units.

P. 034-035

Helmo

Founded in Montreuil in 2007 by Thomas Couderc and Clément vauchez who first met in 1997 during their studies in Besançon, France, Helmo works in various fields including graphic design, posters, signage, book design, and typography mainly for cultural institutions and festivals in France.

P. 106-107, 170-171

Hey

A multidisciplinary design studio based in Barcelona, Spain specialising in brand management and editorial design, packaging and interactive design, Hey shares the profound conviction that good design means combining content, functionality, graphical expression and strategy.

P. 062-063, 102-105, 116-117, 183

Heydays

Based in Oslo, Heydays specialises in printed media, creative direction and graphic design on projects varying from corporate identity, interactive websites, magazines, books and packaging. Heydays strives to find balance between idea, function and aesthetics in every one of them.

P. 076-077

Holt

A Sydney design studio with an established philosophy and a fundmental belief in the role of design in communication and contemporary society offering brand building and award winning design expertise matched to individual requirements of each client.

P. 017, 022-023, 026-027, 197

I LIKE BIRDS

Located in Speicherstadt, Germany, I LIKE BIRDS contemporary design & experimental lab works mainly on posters, books, illustrations, corporate identities and other visual works for cultural and public purposes besides their own projects that include creating fonts, installations, posters, textiles and other crafts produced and published in limited editions.

P. 126-127

Ibanyez, Albert

Born in 1988, the graphic designer at the contemporary art museum Fundació Antoni Tapies since 2010 is passionate about colours and typography.

P. 038-039

Iglesias, Raúl & Latuff Jesús & Novero, Luis

Met at The European Institute of Design and based in Madrid, Spain, the trio has different individual approach to design but shares the same passion for colour and typography.

P. 069

IS Creative Studio.

IS stands for Ingrediente Secreto, that unique "thing" in the soul of anyone driven to create with real passion and originality. Founded by Richars Meza in 2010, the Madrid-based design consultancy delivers print and digital graphics, products and environments for businesses, art institutions and other organisations around the world.

P. 060-061, 094

JJAAKK

The work name of Jesse Kirsch who is the middle sibling of three brothers all sharing the initials JAK. Studied at the School of Visual Arts in New York City, the Portland-based award-winning designer works mainly on packaging, posters and identities creating bold and fun design solutions.

P. 028-029

Kim, Derek

The freelance designer is specialised in identity, typography, and poster design for cultural establishments and small startup companies. Kim also initiates personal projects that allow his creativity to expand into different sectors besides design.

P. 135, 198

Kim, Paul Sangwoo

Graduated in branding and motion graphics from Art Center College of Design in Pasadena, California and now based in Los Angeles, Kim started his career at Prologue Films under Kyle Cooper and is now freelancing at a myriad of studios across all media.

P. 092-093

Kontor Kontur

Working with graphic design, product and interior design in Gothenburg, Kontor Kontur seeks and creates good balance between the refined and the trivial. The team loves to see how objects, people and environments react to and relate to each other.

P. 180-181

Kurppa Hosk

An international interdisciplinary brand and design consultancy specialised in brand and design strategy, corporate identity, art direction, storytelling, retail design, digital design, technology, packaging, product design and user behaviour. Stockholm originated, Kurppa Hosk combines global and local clients, self initiates projects and non-profit assignments, with big agency thinking and studio mentality.

P. 098-099

L2M3 Kommunikationsdesign GmbH

Founded by Sascha Lobe in 1999, the agency handles signage systems and graphic design for exhibitions in addition to traditional tasks like developing corporate images and designing printed matter. The studio has by far received more than 100 international awards in all areas of visual communication.

P. 053

La Tigre

An independent media studio based in Milan directed by designers Luisa Milani and Walter Molteni. Since its opening in 2009, La Tigre takes on a wide variety of projects of different nature, such as web, printing, branding, editing and illustrating.

P. 176-177

Laliberté, Simon

Gratuated in graphic design at UQAM, Montreal, Laliberte founded Atelier BangBang in 2012. It's not only a screen printing workshop for paper and textile but also a design agency and an experimentation lab offering high quality service for a mixed clientele.

P. 030-031

Le Creative Sweatshop

The Paris-based creative studio founded by Mathieu Missiaen, Julien Morin and Stéphane Perrier focuses on fashion, design, contemporary art, and architecture committing to originality, quality and hand-crafted work that constitutes the identity of the trio.

P. 166-167

Lemongraphic

Established in 2007 by Singaporean art director Rayz Ong who specialises in vector illustration, interactive and information design, the multimedia design house is dedicated to help small to medium sized businesses prosper online by offering professional web design and development services.

P. 190-191

Liquorice Studio

Formed in 2009 by Scott Bonanno and now a team of talented individuals whose vast collective experience covers just about every type of communication design service, Liquorice specialises in brand and identity design for print and web for a great mix of clients of all shapes and sizes from corporate, arts, education, hospitality and government sectors.

P. 057

Lo Siento

Graudated at London College of Communication (London Institute) in 2003, Borja Martinez set up the agency in 2004 in Barcelona working in a wide range of projects from packaging, music covers, editorial design, graphic identities for restaurants and film production companies.

P. 169

macmeier

The private platform of Martin Meier collaborating with people on smaller projects or explorations besides being a consultant at IDEO working on all kinds of strategic and exciting challenges.

P. 168

Mad Keen Design & Art Direction

Founded by Ryan Dixon who is a UK based designer with a minimal and visually simplistic style. Striking colour and well structured typography are the key to his work.

P. 188-189

Mellier, Fanette

Born in 1977 and graduated in 2000 at the École supérieure des arts décoratifs in Strasbourg, Mellier worked with graphic talents like Pierre Di Sciullo and Pierre Bernard before she started as an independent graphic designer in 2004. Works mainly on prints for publishing firms, her work has been exhibited in numerous contemporary art museums and centers such as the Centre Pompidou in Paris, France.

P. 220-221

Metaklinika

Located in Belgrade, Metaklinika works mainly on branding, graphic design, photography, exhibition design, illustration and motion graphics. Founded by photographer Dušan Đorđević, illustrator Lazar Bodroža, and graphic designer Nenad Trifunović, the studio has done a large number of campaigns in fields of culture and higher business providing unusual and fresh solutions.

P. 142

Midnight Rendez-Vous

Behind the brand is the wild and crazy creator, Renaud, who however looks shy and sagacious in appearance. Drawing inspiration from the clash between materials, Renaud creates uniquely cool, eccentric, and extravagant clothing for "quirky stylish" nights.

P. 158-161

Mind Design

Based in London, the independent graphic design studio founded by Holger Jacobs after graduating from the Royal College of Art in 1999, is specialised in visual identities and has worked for a wide range of clients in different sectors.

P. 074-075

Mutabor Design GmbH

Offering multi-channel brand design and creative brand management in all dimensions to develop holistic brand presences that is substantial and integrated, the interdisciplinary team believes in brand story that is able to tell, experience, move.

P. 058-059

My Wet Calvin

Consisting architect and graphic-web designer Leonidas Ikonomou and preschool educator Aris Nikolopoulos, the creative noisy pop duo from Greece's local indie scene overtaking the majority of the visual projects related to the band such as record covers, posters, websites, music videos, concert and other promotional artifacts. Besides the DIY practices and amateur ethos, they are also involved in high-end projects and have received awards and honorary mentions at the Greek Graphic Design Awards 2008-09.

P. 061

Novembre, Fabio

Born in 1966 with a background in movie direction and architecture, Novembre opened his own studio in Milan in 1994. From 2000-2003, he was also the art director at Bisazza working with Cappellini, Driade, Meritalia, Flaminia and Casamania. Since 2008, he has been invited to exhibit his work by numerous national museums like the Triennale Design Museum of Milan and the Italian Pavillion at the 2009 Shanghai Expo on behalf of the Comune of Milan.

P. 236-241

Palatre et Leclere Architectes

Founded by Olivier Palatre and Tiphaine Leclere in 2006, the agency works in both public and private sectors on projects of different nature including housing, offices, hospitals, cinema, schools. They are a finalist of "Le Moniteur" in 2011 for the project of the Second Chance school.

P. 248-249

Palma, Paolo

Since 1999, Palma joined Fabrica, the Benetton group's communication research centre, with which he still works as a consultant there today. In 2006, Palma co-founded and has been the art director of Heads Collective, an international design and communication studio, which develops projects in different creative fields and disciplines. Since 2011, Palma has become a professor of graphic design at ISIA (Higher Institute for Artistic Industries) in Urbino, Italy.

P. 196

Pan, Kerstin zu

A Berlin based photographer who has worked her craft in unusual circumstances, blurring the boundaries between fashion photography and high art by combining the languages of various media.

www.kerstinzupan.com

P. 200-203

Penique productions

A group of artists of different disciplines that realises temporary facilities, Penique productions is founded by Sergi Arbusà, Pablo Baqué, Chamo San, and Pol Clusella and now with offices in Barcelona, Spain, Rio de Janeiro, Brazil, and London, UK.

P. 242-245

Pentagram

One of the world's largest independent design consultancy founded in 1972 running by 19 partners. With offices in London, New York, San Francisco, Austin and Berlin, the firm specialises in different areas of graphic design, industrial design and architecture, producing printed materials, environments, products and interactive media for a wide range of international clients.

P. 014-015

Peregrín, Paco

Currently residing in Madrid, the Mediterranean photographer works across the globe in fashion, beauty, art and advertising for brands such as Nike, Adidas, Toyota, Diesel and Carlsberg. His work has been featured in international publications including Vogue, Harper's Bazaar, and Elle and numerous exhibitions around the world. In 2008, Paco was awarded first place in the National Professional Photography Awards in Spain.

P. 150-151

Podhajsky, Leif

Working to explore and utilise themes of connectedness, the relevance of nature and the psychedelic or altered experience, the artist and creative director creates artwork for a number of bands and record labels like Warp Records, Modular Records, Sony Music, etc. and has exhibited work in the UK, Berlin, The Netherlands, Sydney and Melbourne.

P. 096-097

Post Projects

The Vancouver based graphic design studio founded by Alex Nelson and Beau House focusing on creative projects that include identity and branding, print media, and interactive development.

P. 084-085

Present & Correct

Opened its virtual doors in 2008 aiming to share the long-term obsession with stationery, paper and office objects inspired by homework, post offices and schools, P&C offers an online shopping wonderland for their original design products as well as other international designers', alongside vintage items collected from Europe.

P. 108-109, 118-121

Purpose

A graphic design consultancy committed to producing design that promotes clarity and creates design that helps people to communicate more effectively. Purpose creates visual identities, print, exhibition and pack designs for a variety of clients, from individuals to global organisations.

P. 140-141

R.I.S. Projects

Angelique Piliere and Lee Owens met while studying graphic design and began working together after moving to London in 2006. Their work is a mixture of mixed media collage, illustration, type creation and design. Opened in the beginning of 2012, R.I.S. Projects works within all areas of art direction, identity, web, and print design.

P. 144-145

Raffinerie AG für Gestaltung

Established in 2000, the studio is managed by Reto Ehrbar, Nenad Kovačić and Christian Haas with a talented team of graphic artists and illustrators.

P. 210-211

Raw Color

The collaboration between Christoph Brach and Daniera ter Haar based in Eindhoven. The duo displays a desire to conduct primary research and question meanings driven by curiosity. Their work reflect a sophisticated treatment of material by mixing the fields of photography and graphic design.

P. 072-073, 184-187

Resort Studio

Founded in 2012 by Michael Häne and Dieter Glauser, both studied at the Zürich University of the Arts, Resort conceives and designs identities, digital media and printed matter for companies, institutions and individuals with a cultural or economic background.

P. 054

Reynolds and Reyner

With a fundamental belief in the power of design, Reynolds and Reyner sees design not only a way to make modern and high quality design but an approach to process whereas result will serve as the basis of communications between brand and consumers.

P. 078-081

Saxow, Matilda

A Swedish graphic designer and art director based in London predominantly engaged with editorial design and branding projects for the cultural and commercial industries.

P. 146-147

SEA

An award winning brand communications agency working across all media and disciplines from brand strategy and positioning, corporate identity, brand art direction and digital Media, SEA works for international clients such as Adidas, Selfridges, Jamie Oliver, EMI, Matthew Williamson, King Sturge, Global Cool and Maitland.

P. 050-051, 065, 086-089

Second Story Interactive Studios

The pioneer of new interactive experiences connecting brands and institutions to their customers, guests, and audiences through inventive blends of technology and storytelling in venues and across digital channels.

P. 208-209

Studio Brave

Specialised in brand communication, the guiding vision of the studio comes from their name where brave thinking leads to unexpected outcomes.

P. 082-083

Studio Dumbar

Expertised in strategy, communication, branding and process-management, the international agency with a Dutch heritage works for a variety of clients big and small, from business and government to cultural and non-profit. Founded by Gert Dumbar in Hague in 1977 and now based in Rotterdam leading by Liza Enebeis, Karmen Kekic and Tom Dorresteijn, the agency has a close working relationship with Joost Roozekrans and Zou Zhengfang in Shanghai (2005), and Simon Park in Seoul (2012).

P. 070-071

Studio Iknoki

Based in Italy, the visual design and communication studio works within different fields of design from visual identity to editorial and digital projects for clients including institutions and businesses big and small.

P. 195

Studio Laucke Siebein

Focusing on creative strategy, dynamic identities, graphic, book and web design, the design studio based in Amsterdam and Berlin has received numerous awards including the Art Directors Club Award NY and The European Design Award. Their work has been presented in magazines such as Grafik, Novum, and a large number of books. In addition to daily design practice, the two founders - Dirk Laucke and Johanna Siebein are visiting tutors at the Hochschule für Künste Bremen, Germany and give lectures and workshops internationally.

P. 165

Studio Lin

The NYC based graphic design practice of Alex Lin exploring new territory through challenging collaborations with creative visionaries in the fields of architecture, industrial design, art and fashion, their work is a highly defined rationale but not a singular style.

www.studiolin.org
P. 056

Studio mw

Founded by Jeanne Moinon and Pierre-Olivier Thiriet in 2009 in Paris' suburb, the graphic studio focuses on printed design for public, private and institutional partners in addition to artistic collaborations and experimental researches creating a conceptual impression echoing to personal graphic sensibilities.

P. 164

Studio wilfredtimo

The collaboration between a young graphic design duo Wilfred van der Weide (1984) and Timo Demollin (1988), living and working in Utrecht, The Netherlands. The studio focuses on communicating through research in material and the use of archetypical shapes and symbols.

P. 192-193

Acknowledgements

We would like to thank all the designers and companies who have involved in the production of this book. This project would not have been accomplished without their significant contribution to the compilation of this book. We would also like to express our gratitude to all the producers for their invaluable opinions and assistance throughout this entire project. The successful completion also owes a great deal to many professionals in the creative industry who have given us precious insights and comments. And to the many others whose names are not credited but have made specific input in this book, we thank you for your continuous support the whole time.

Future Editions

If you wish to participate in viction:ary's future projects and publications, please send your website or portfolio to submit@victionary.com